VIRGINIA ARCHITECTURE
IN THE SEVENTEENTH CENTURY

LECTOR HOUSE PUBLIC DOMAIN WORKS

VIRGINIA ARCHITECTURE IN THE SEVENTEENTH CENTURY

HENRY CHANDLEE FORMAN

ISBN: 978-93-90015-91-7

Published: -

© 2020
LECTOR HOUSE LLP

LECTOR HOUSE LLP
E-MAIL: lectorpublishing@gmail.com

VIRGINIA ARCHITECTURE
IN THE SEVENTEENTH CENTURY

BY

HENRY CHANDLEE FORMAN
Ph.D. (Fine Arts), A.I.A.

WITH DRAWINGS AND PHOTOGRAPHS BY THE AUTHOR

DEDICATED TO
SINGLETON PEABODY MOOREHEAD

CONTENTS

LIST OF ILLUSTRATIONS

INTRODUCTION

In the green, southern land which today comprises the Commonwealth of Virginia, there flourished three centuries ago the fine art of architecture, and it is with that subject—the art of building in good design, with sound construction, and for the proper use—that this brief essay is concerned. But it is deplorable for one interested in the subject of historic preservation to have to relate what time and man have done to seventeenth-century Virginia architecture; there is so very little left compared to what formerly existed. If it has not been man himself with his so-called "improvements," his neglect, and his vandalism, it has been fire, the weather, and the insects which have caused widespread obliteration—almost a clean sweep—of the structures of those times.

Nevertheless, by means of careful studies of a few existing buildings, of several foundations under the ground, of artifacts and manuscripts, of old prints and photographs—and even of relevant material found in Britain,—we possess today enough data to make a goodly outline of the subject. Set forth here are the principal styles of architecture in Virginia between 1600 and 1700, with some account of their origins and their development.

PUNCHED BRASS KEY ESCUTCHEON

$2\frac{5}{8}$" long, from the "Bin House," Jamestown

The writer has endeavored to approach this task with understanding and sympathy, for which he is qualified. He has lived on the Jamestown road in Williamsburg and has Jamestown in his blood; he has written and lectured much on Virginia; is currently a registered architect in that Commonwealth; and on both sides of his family traces his descent back to the seventeenth-century Chews,

Brents, Ayres, and Skipwiths, who, living along the banks of the James River, saw much of the architecture described herein. In the preparation for this little work, two incidents stand out as being important and essential: in 1936 he was a house guest of the Association for the Preservation of Virginia Antiquities and lived in its "Malvern Hill" reproduction at Jamestown while he made studies of the ruins on that property; and in 1940 he stayed several nights on the Pamunkey Indian Reservation, near West Point, as guest of those Virginia Indians, while he made a study in art and archaeology in part preparation for the doctorate.

This work is protected under the copyright law of the United States of America, and no part of this work may be taken or used in any fashion—whether text or illustration—without written permission from the publishers and the author.

We commence the fascinating story of the early architecture of Virginia by describing the first architectural style which ever flourished there—a style about which most people know little and most school children nothing.

VIRGINIA ARCHITECTURE IN THE SEVENTEENTH CENTURY

I

FIRST IN VIRGINIA: AMERICAN INDIAN ARCHITECTURE

When the first English colonists arrived before Jamestown Island, Virginia, on May 13, 1607, there was already in existence an indigenous architecture which had been flourishing in that land for hundreds of years. It is true that that particular kind of architecture, American Indian, was, by and large, a perishable wooden one; nevertheless, the subject may not be ignored by stating that it did not exist. This Indian art of building forms an important chapter in the early history of Virginia.

For thousands of years the Indian—a light-brown man, with brown or black eyes, and straight, blue-black hair—was the owner of what is now the United States of America. That he roamed the country which is now called Virginia for "countless centuries" is proven by the ancient Folsom spear points—one of red jasper—discovered among the Peaks of Otter, near the Skyline Drive, Bedford County, Virginia. And the Indians who made those spear points lived thirteen thousand or more years ago.

The Indian tribes who settled east of the Mississippi River became skilful in mound-building, sculpture, and other accomplishments. They were generally clever and dexterous peoples. In the areas covered by Virginia and the other southeastern states the life of the natives had an exotic flavor. Their graceful and courtly manner was noted by the first European explorers.

At the time of the white settlement in 1607, the land of Virginia was occupied by three main linguistic groups: first, the *Algonquian*, which included the Powhatan Confederacy in tidewater north of the James River, and the gentle Accowmacks and Accohannocks on the Eastern Shore; second, the *Siouan*, located in Piedmont Virginia above the falls of the James, that is, west of Richmond—a group of Indians which included the Monacan and Manahoac Confederacies; third, the *Iroquoian*, which included the Cherokees and the Nottaways, both tribes of which lived south and southeast of the James River.

In 1607 there were altogether about 17,000 Indians in Virginia between the mountains and the sea. It has been estimated that they lived in about two hundred settlements, called "towns," and in some four thousand dwelling-houses.

Their architecture, as has been mentioned, was for the most part a perishable one. At this time, three hundred and fifty years after 1607, not one American Indian wooden structure has remained above Virginia ground. By such complete destruction we and our descendants are forever deprived of the physical background which would continuously remind us of the Indian past, in the way that the city of Rome reminds Italians of their Roman past.

I. THE TOWNS

In the Old Dominion, Indian towns were small, usually covering about an acre of ground and containing ten or twelve buildings—seldom more than thirty. They were always built on or near a river or other body of water. One of these settlements by the name of "Kecoughtan," the present Hampton, possessed in 1607 only eighteen Indian buildings.

The towns themselves may be grouped into three kinds: open, fortified, and partially fortified.

The first group, the open towns, comprised those settlements which were laid out irregularly, with the buildings generally arranged loosely on either side of a central avenue or cleared space. Footpaths criss-crossed this open area.

The fortified or walled towns were, as far as is known, built on two designs, round and square. The chief constructional method of fortification was the palisade-and-moat, or to put it another way, the stockade-and-ditch. This architectural arrangement, it may be mentioned, was employed by some of the peoples of prehistoric Europe, and by the Romans, and Anglo-Saxons, and others abroad. But the American Indian developed the method entirely independently of Europeans.

The palisades thus built by the Indians in Virginia usually were tree trunks or heavy timbers, from five inches to eight in diameter. Sometimes, as at "Patawomeke" or "Potomac" village, the posts were only three to four inches across. Corner posts were generally larger, being ten inches thick or thereabouts. The timbers, usually with the branches uncut, were for the most part set vertically in the bank of earth thrown up by excavating the moat or trench. They reached two or three feet underground, and rose seven to twelve feet above the earth. At times, the posts leaned outward to make scaling them more difficult. The ditch was usually outside the palisade.

Often these heavy timbers were set close enough to touch each other, when they are called "palisading." At other times, they were placed in the ground a little apart from one another, the interstices being filled with branches and the bark of trees interwoven, and with bullrush mats, to make the fortification spear-and-arrow proof. This method of construction we call puncheoning. In other words, the stockade comprised "puncheons" which were matted and "wattled"—"wattling" being the term for the basketry type of weaving of branches and bark strips. When the posts of a fort were wattled six inches apart, it was comparatively easy for the defenders to shoot through cracks in the wattling.

A variation of the palisade method was the twisting and interweaving of the top branches of the tree-posts into a tight mass, in order to discourage climbers. For observation and defense, loopholes at a convenient distance from each other were usually inserted in the walls.

Not all Indian palisades were substantial. Perhaps some became too ancient for their own good. Great storms might blow them down on a dark night. At one Siouan village, "the first Puff blew down all the Palisadoes that fortified the town." As a result, some fortifications had their palisades doubled or trebled for strength. Other fortified settlements were erected like a nest of walls, one within the other.

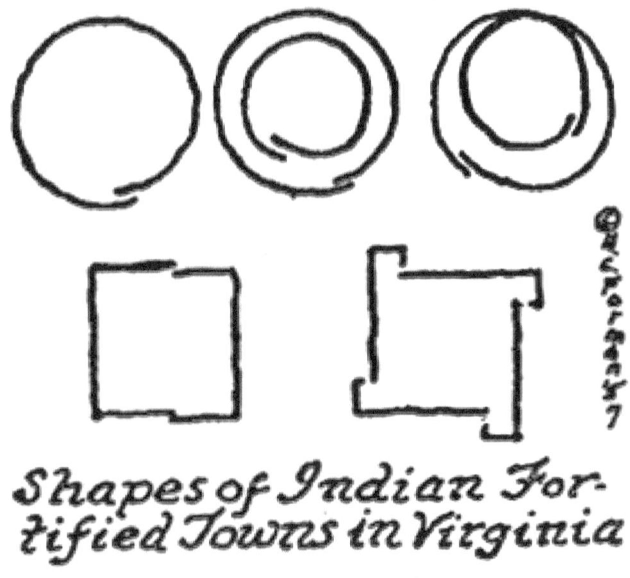

Shapes of Indian Fortified Towns in Virginia

Circular towns, like Paski, in Southampton County, Virginia, usually had in the center a ceremonial space firebed. Separate buildings were grouped about that area. In order to protect the inhabitants against attack, the usual entrance in the walls was narrow, so that only one man at a time could enter. Often measuring two-and-a-half feet wide, such a gateway was formed, snail-shell-like, by the overlapping of the ends of the palisade. When the English in Virginia saw such gates, they called them "turnpikes," possibly because the gates carried spears or sharp projections, vaguely resembling the spiked entrances of medieval England.

The plan of another circular settlement, "Patawomeke" or "Potomac," in Stafford County, Virginia, is of interest because there were two rings of palisaded posts, not concentric, but with the rings touching each other at one point. The inner ring was about one hundred seventy-five feet in diameter, and the outer two hundred and eighty.

Square towns, like the Nottaway settlement, also in Southampton County, usually measured from two hundred to three hundred feet on a side, and had more than one palisaded entrance. Though not yet proven, it is believed that when the Indians employed "flankers," which are side or corner projections, or bastions, in their walls, as they did upon occasion, they copied them from the English settlers.

The third class of town, the partially fortified, was very common. The chief building and a few structures would be enclosed, leaving the remainder unprotected outside the walls.

II. THE MOUNDS

The Indian earth mounds in the land of Virginia have not perished as rapidly as the wooden buildings, with the result that many mounds have survived in one fashion or another. They are of at least three kinds: the burial mound, the platform mound, and the effigy mound. But it must be admitted that to this date, as far as research has disclosed, examples of the last two categories have not yet been identified.

By far the greater number of mounds were located in Piedmont Virginia, above the Falls of the James. Unlike the Siouan and the Iroquoian, the Algonquian tribes of tidewater Virginia, such as the Powhatans, did not erect earth mounds — at least, as far as present evidence indicates. The earliest white American to have explored scientifically a Virginia mound was Thomas Jefferson. A few years before the American Revolution, he excavated and examined a burial mound on the Rivanna River in Albemarle County, and found it to be a communal grave with an estimated one thousand skeletons laid in distinct strata. The structure was spheroidal in shape, and about forty feet in diameter. Its original height was thought to be twice the height of a man.

Such a burial mound was made gradually by covering with earth and stone one skeleton lying on the ground, then placing a second skeleton on top and again covering with earth and stone, until in that manner a thousand burials had been made. A similar mound, but larger, was found beside the Rapidan River, in Orange County. Many earth mounds have been found west of the Shenandoah River.

Within this burial mound classification may be included the "cairn," a Gaelic name meaning "the heap," and comprising a grave under a small pile of stones. The largest of such rock heaps is said to be fifteen feet in diameter and three feet high. Several small cairns have been located on the banks of the Rivanna.

As for platform mounds, it was the custom of the Cherokee tribe to erect such elevated earth forms as sub-structures or bases for wooden temples or council chambers. As has been already indicated, some Cherokees lived in the land of Virginia, notably in the vicinity of the Peaks of Otter, in Bedford County. Further south, as far away as Georgia, some platform mounds are immense, man-made hills, formerly covered with smooth, polished, hard clay, which at times reflected the rays of the sun. Great buildings once stood upon the summits of those mounds. Because none have hitherto been discovered in the Cherokee area of Virginia does not mean that none existed. And the same can be said of the Cherokee effigy mounds.

An effigy mound is one built for religious purposes, generally in the shape or silhouette of an animal or bird; but as yet, none has been discovered in Virginia. The probability that there were effigy mounds is strong.

III. DWELLING-HOUSES

Contrary to popular belief, the Indians of Virginia were not a tent people. They lived in wigwams, which are *houses*. Tents belonged to the natives of the Great Plains, like the Sioux Indians.

Among the various types of wigwams there are two chief kinds: the circular or "beehive" dwelling, and the rectangular or "arbor" house. Both of these names were given by the English settlers because the buildings resembled constructions in their own homeland across the sea.

The round house had a domed roof. On the other hand, the "arbor" abode resembled, in the words of the English, "the arbories in our gardens in England." The roofs of such habitations were arched in the form of a tunnel vault.

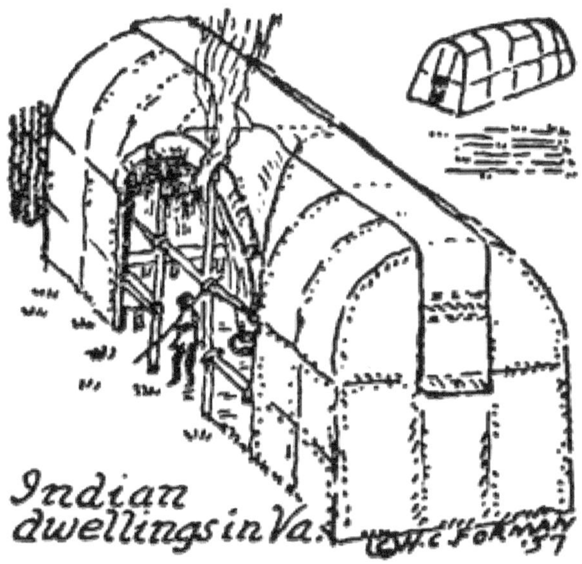

The construction of the wigwam was generally a framework of saplings or young trees spaced nearly vertically in the ground at regular intervals, and bowed at the top, to make the dome or tunnel vault, as the case might be. Although the saplings were usually tied securely at the top with "withes"—which are flexible twigs,—and with roots, vines, reeds, or bark strips, some dwellings had young trees long enough to have both ends stuck in the ground, so that nothing had to be tied at the top. Ordinarily for strength the walls of such homes were battered or sloped inward at the top.

At all events, cross pieces of small poles, running horizontally, were fastened to the saplings in order to serve as braces and as supports for the various kinds of curtain material employed by the Indians—materials like woven-grass mats, bark, and skins.

One of the curious features of some of these arbor houses which the writer does not believe to have been elsewhere described before, is the use of a kind of "lunette" or half-moon window, of multiple lights, on the long side of a domicile. Such a feature gave additional ceiling space and more headroom. If lunettes were employed opposite each other on each side of a wigwam roof, for which arrangement we have no evidence, the roof must have resembled what we call a "cross-vault." It is interesting that lunettes and cross-vaults of masonry were employed by the Romans and the Goths of Europe. That the Indian had lunettes and probably had cross-vaults was a mere coincidence.

It seems that most of the arbor houses averaged twelve feet wide and eighteen long, according to finds made in excavations. Even so, many lodgings were longer. Some were over seventy feet, and were divided into separate compartments by interior partitions of saplings and mats.

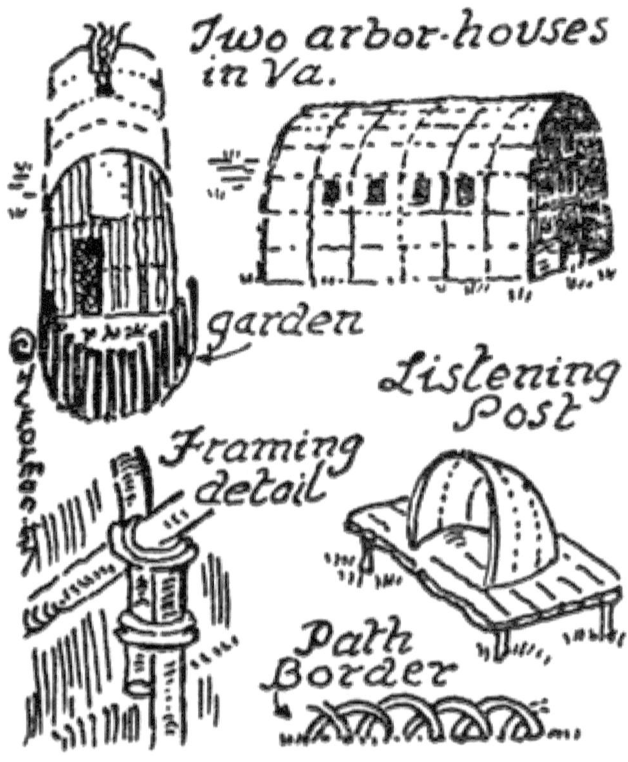

For wigwams the covering mats were woven with long rushes or grasses, and for the most part extended from the top of the house to the ground. They were usually three or four feet wide and in length eight or ten feet, and were stitched together or to the framework of the dwelling. Furthermore, mats were not the only covering employed. Bark of cedar, oak, or hickory was used, and made a thicker and better insulated material than mats, which in summer permitted the interiors to heat up like stoves. The bark was stripped off the tree in great flakes, and was laid so closely together that no rain could enter. Some wigwams had a combination of mat and bark, like mat walls and bark roofs. And sometimes animal skins were used as coverings.

As for house entrances, the beehive had one doorway, the arbor abode usually one at each end. The "doors" were usually mats, which could be rolled up neatly in hot weather. Often in winter curtains of bear skins would cover the doorways.

The Indians anticipated the present outdoor-, glass-wall-, and barbecue-loving age by arranging their wigwams so that in warm weather the sidewall mats could be rolled up on the sapling framework, much as the flaps of a circus tent can be raised. Consequently, in the Indian dwelling one or more whole sides could be opened to balmy breezes, throwing the whole interior construction open to outside gaze.

The place for the fire was the firebed, and it stood in the ground in the center of the wigwam. When the lodging was long, there was usually a fireplace for each compartment. Flues there were none. The smoke from the fire, winding its way leisurely around the interior, finally found its way through an outlet or louvre in the roof or through windows at the eaves level. In wet weather a mat flap or piece of bark would cover the louvre. On the other hand, in the summer time, the Indian enjoyed cooking over an outdoor firebed in true barbecue style.

The wigwam windows were merely apertures without glass—true "windholes." They comprised single, double, triple, or quadruple lights, sometimes arranged in "lunette" fashion, as has been indicated. To keep out bad weather, these openings had moveable covers, like bark shutters; but the prevailing method seems to have been to run long mats, either lengthwise or crosswise, over the arbor roof, so that the ends of the mats formed covering flaps.

It is interesting to note that the Indian knew that smoky rooms were undesirable, so that when he could obtain them, logs of pine were burned, a process which cut down the amount of smoke. On rare occasions when the fire went out, he lit pine splinter "candles," of which he generally kept a large stock on hand.

When he went journeying apace, he rolled heavy logs against the doorways to keep out wild beasts and marauders.

Possibly because the American Indian was a descendant of Orientals, he was accustomed to little in the way of furniture. Chairs and tables he appears to have had none. The ground was stable and permanent. An important chief might have, however, a low earth bench covered with skins, for comfort. But the rest of the people sat on the ground or upon their "beds." It should be written here that the whites were not the first on this side of the Atlantic to use built-in furniture. The

Indian invented built-in beds, which were turned into benches in the daytime. They were made by thrusting forked sticks into the ground, about a foot or two in height, to support a horizontal framework of small poles, tied to the saplings of the wigwam itself. Over that framework were stretched skins, furs, coarse mats, and sometimes soft white grass mats of excellent quality and handsome patterns. Great men, like the "Emperor" Powhatan, had leather pillows, a real luxury. In their arrangement the built-in beds were in the arbor houses placed generally end-to-end along two or three sides. Again, if there were plenty of space, the beds were separated one from another, but still abutted the walls. In the beehive dwellings the beds circled the fire.

One feature which we today remember in our old-fashioned homes is the pantry or buttery; but the Indian habitation was not even "modern" enough for that. There was no native pantry. Food contained in woven sacks, gourds, and like receptacles, was hung from the cross-beams high above the heads of the occupants of the wigwam.

IV. KING'S HOUSES, TREASURE HOUSES, AND TEMPLES

The lodging of a "werowance" or chief, or of an "emperor," who was head of many chiefs, was called by the English a "King's House" or "Palace." It was commonly an enlarged arbor house, "broad and long," sometimes with winding interior passages. The principal residence of Powhatan was at Portan or Powhatan Bay, on York River, and was of the arbor variety and very long. Another King's House, dating about 1649, on the Eastern Shore of Virginia, had a framework of great locust posts sunk in the ground at the corners and at the partitions, and the arched roof was tied to the framework by vines and roots. In breadth this "Palace" was some sixty feet long and eighteen or twenty wide. The bed platforms, each about six feet long, were placed on the long sides of the edifice, and were separated from each other by some five feet. In the center was the customary firebed. The Eastern Shore potentate himself sat upon a bank of earth adorned with finely-dressed deer skins, and with the very best otter and beaver skins which could be found in that region.

As in the ordinary dwelling-house, the entire wall of mats and coverings could be rolled up as high as the King should desire.

In size, the Treasure House of Powhatan, at a place called Orapaks, was one of the largest known structures in seventeenth-century Virginia. According to accounts, it reached somewhere between one hundred fifty and one hundred eighty feet in length.

That some of these immense buildings were not without ornament is proven by the description of the sculptured corner posts of the Orapaks Treasure House. There were figures resembling a bear, leopard, dragon, and giant man. Another popular architectural sculpture was the bird, such as eagle, which was set upon great Indian edifices.

The "Mortuary Temple," sometimes called by the English the "Temple," "Temple-Tomb," or "Bone-House," seems to have been the most interesting of their known wooden edifices. To the Indians such a structure was a "Quacasum House," because it contained idols or "quioccos." Some of those images of their gods were ornate, being hand-carved and painted, dressed with beads, copper, and necklaces, and adorned with skins. Sometimes the idols were placed under a matted canopy in the same way that the Madonnas of some of the Old Masters abroad sat under canopies with "cloths of honor" behind them.

A Central Type of Indian Temple in Virginia

The interior of the Mortuary Temple was dark and mysterious. The only light, it seems, came through a single doorway. Some of these sanctums were arbor-like, but others were built on a central plan: round, hexagonal, or octagonal. We know that the roof of at least one Temple was an ogee-pointed, "gored" dome. An ogee is a line of double curvature, and the silhouette of such a dome was curved in that manner.

At Pamunkey, Virginia, Powhatan possessed three Temples, situated on top of red sandy hills—which, by the way, may have been artificial platform mounds. Each structure was built arbor-wise, and reached nearly sixty feet in length. Others of the same ilk extended in length as much as one hundred feet. Like the treasure houses, they had a circle of carved posts surrounding them, upon which the native sculptors could make ornate and colorful carvings.

The chief function of the Temple was a temporary storage place for the important dead, before permanent burial in ossuaries or mounds. The bodies were stuffed mummies with bones and skin still intact, and were laid out side by side upon a scaffolding of vertical poles about nine or ten feet high, well lined with mats, and roofed with a matted tunnel vault. Such a scaffolding under the temple roof formed a kind of miniature arbor home for the deceased. As in ordinary dwellings, the mats of the scaffolding could be rolled up at will. Beneath the platform lived priests, who had charge of the dead and who were reported to have spent their time mumbling incantations night and day.

It seems to have been customary to orient the temple doorway, that is, to place it on the eastern side, and to build, as in the king's houses, dark and labyrinthine passageways, located in the west end of the sanctum, where stood two or three "black" idols, facing eastward.

V. BATH HOUSES AND OTHER BUILDINGS

The English called the Indian bath house by the names of "Bagnio" and "Sweating House." Such fabrics were generally circular, like the outdoor ovens used by the Indians, and had no windows. The Siouan tribes of Virginia built some of their bath houses of stone; but throughout Virginia the common material for such structures was wood. As in the ordinary dwelling, regularly-spaced saplings were thrust into the ground and bowed overhead. Then the interstices were close-ly woven with branches—that is, wattled,—and were plastered with mud.

The Indian took what amounted to a Turkish bath, a method still in use in Finland, Mexico, and other parts of the world. But in Virginia the bath went like this: the bather heated ten or twelve small or "pebble" stones in a fire. When they had become red hot, they were placed in a firebed inside the "Bagnio." The bather then stripped, grabbed a blanket, and shut the door. Slowly pouring water upon the hot stones, he caused steam to rise so thick you could cut it with a knife. He sat on a bench until he could no longer stand the intense heat, at which moment he rushed out of the bath house and jumped into the river, over his head and ears. If the bather happened to be ill, he was supposed to be washed clean of sickness. At any rate that was the way of taking the Saturday night bath on the James, the York, the Pamunkey, the Rivanna, and elsewhere in the Old Dominion.

* * * * *

Other structures known to have been built by the Indian in Virginia were hunting houses, platforms, fences, landings, and outdoor ceremonial centers.

Many were the weeks that the Indian left logs rolled in front of his house door and was off hunting or foraging. On long trips he erected "hunting houses," tem-porary shelters also known as "camping stations." These were probably simplified wigwams, which could be easily taken down and reërected in another place.

In every town there stood "scaffolding" or raised platforms, where the inhabi-tants frequently sat and conversed, and which served somewhat the same purpose as our own outdoor summerhouses of olden times. But the Indian platforms had a loft made of hurdles, upon which the women of the settlement placed their maize, fish, and other foods to dry.

There was another kind of platform, constructed in their tilled fields, to serve as scarecrows to their crops of beans, pompions, tomatoes, squash, corn, and the like. Upon the platform was built a small cabin or cottage, sometimes arranged in the shape of a half-dome, like a "round chair," in which an Indian sat to watch the fields. Such listening posts anticipated our own radar warning installations.

The usual fence was a row of irregular pales, but sometimes it was made of wattles. A rarer kind, it seems, was a low fence to border paths which comprised overlapping semi-circles of tree branches. We today have the same kind of staggered semi-circles for our park paths, but they are usually made of iron, which the Indian did not possess.

Nothing appears to be known of the form of the Indian dock or wharf, like the "Indian Landing" of 1654 on the Harmanson tract in Accomack County; but their bridges were generally simple constructions comprising forked stakes with poles laid across them for a footway. Because there were no wheeled vehicles, footpaths and foot bridges for land travel were sufficient. For that matter, the main highway was the water.

In this connection, the oldest "road" in Virginia, called by the English "the Greate Road," which ran from James City to Middle Plantation, now Williamsburg, was at first—at least in the Jamestown-Pasbyhayes section of it—an Indian pathway. In the beginning the English called it a "bridle" path.

The open-air ceremonial centers, to which the English gave the name of "Dancing Grounds," played an important part in Indian life. To the native the art of dancing was essential to his religion. The usual large space was layed out for dances and bounded by a circle of wooden posts, sculptured with painted heads. At one center the English likened such carven figures to the faces of veiled nuns. Other posts sometimes had men's countenances upon them.

VI. UNUSUAL CONSTRUCTIONS

At the native town of Sapponey, Brunswick County, Virginia, there was an interesting variation of the usual town plan. The dwellings were row houses, adjoining one another in the form of a circle. The individual home had palisaded walls, made of large, squared timbers, set two feet deep in the earth and rising seven feet above it. The back walls of such habitations formed the town wall, and there were three entrances into the settlement, formed by leaving passageways about six feet wide between certain pairs of buildings. But the most unusual feature was that the abodes possessed pitched or gable roofs, built with rafters. Upon the rafters hickory bark strips were set so closely together that no rain could penetrate.

Another Indian habitation with pitched roof and palisaded walls once stood in a spot north of the present Pamunkey Indian Reservation, near West Point, Virginia. Still another native homestead, it seems, had puncheoned walls with a low-pitched roof of unusual construction: each half of the roof was hinged at the ridge and could be raised like a flap in order to obtain better ventilation.

Perhaps the Indian obtained the idea of a pitched roof from the whites, but that theory is open to question. We know that, among other good qualities, the native had an inventive mind. It is difficult for some of us to realize that some Virginia Indians employed plastered ceilings in their dwelling-houses, but that is exactly how the Cherokees of Virginia constructed their ceilings—the plaster being the usual combination of clay and straw.

* * * * *

The first chapter in Virginia's architectural history—the Indian chapter—is one of which we may be proud, because, in spite of its widespread perishable nature, the architecture was well-designed, beautifully ornamented, and often of great size and dignity. It, too, sometimes revealed the native's inventive tendencies. No one can relegate with justice the status of Indian architecture to a lower place when the Orapaks Treasure House of Powhatan had a larger floor area than that of the greatest mansion of all Virginia in the seventeenth century—Sir William Berkeley's home, "The Green Spring," near Jamestown—which is shown in our diagram without the "ell" addition. Even with the "ell" included, the Orapaks Treasure House was larger. Moreover, this Treasure House was more extensive in ground space than the largest English house of its time in the American colonies—Lord Baltimore's "Governor's Castle," St. Mary's City, Maryland, of 1639.

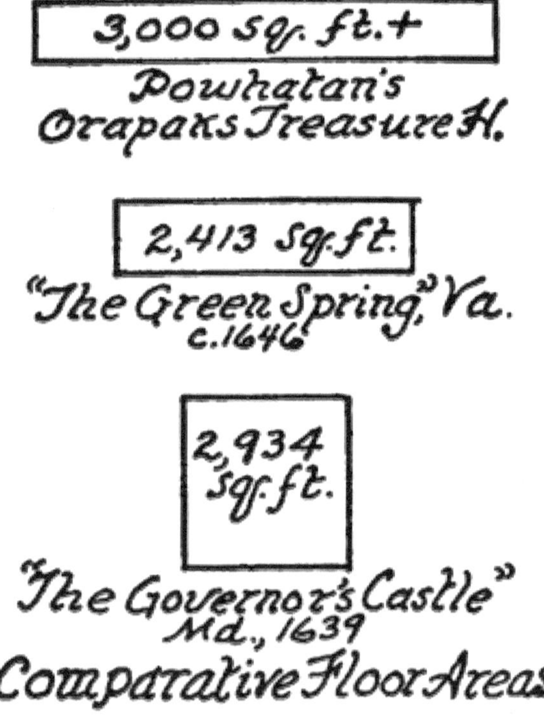

The Cherokees of Virginia may have had, and probably did have, council chambers larger than the Orapaks Treasure House, similar to the great town house holding five hundred persons, which the Cherokees constructed at Chote in Tennessee.

Of this fact we may be sure: the Cherokees were great builders. They comprised a nation extending from Virginia to Georgia, and only a century and a half ago they possessed their own written language, their own dictionary, and their own printed newspaper. It was from that Cherokee nation that Will Rogers descended, and it was Rogers' great uncle, Chief Joseph Vann, who built for himself in 1803 in the Georgia mountains a large brick mansion, with a handsome hanging staircase and tall panelled mantels and richly-carved cornices with rosettes. It is a manor house after the English fashion; but in the attic are two incipient, rounded, Indian council chambers with sapling partitions—because an Indian is always an Indian. It has been this writer's good fortune to restore Vann's mansion for the State. But how could a mere Indian, our school children will say, build a manor equal to that of a white man? The Cherokees could.

* * * * *

Thirty-seven years before the English established Jamestown, a Spanish Jesuit and other missionaries from Florida erected (1570), according to the best authority, a hut and small chapel in the James-York region of what later became Virginia. These buildings may have resembled the crude St. Augustine mission of 1566, the earliest Spanish church in this country, which was constructed of vertical plank walls and with a gable roof. No trace of these two structures has ever been found, but they constitute a short Spanish chapter in the history of early Virginia architecture.

II

THE ENGLISH VERNACULAR AT A GLANCE

As we have seen, the first English colonists, arriving in 1607 from across the sea, to construct James Fort in Virginia, encountered a native architecture flourishing about them. In establishing that outpost in the New World, which was to become the first permanent English settlement on this side of the Atlantic, as well as the beginning of the British Empire—now the Commonwealth,—they brought with them a knowledge of, and skill in, English architecture. At that time, the beginning of the seventeenth century, architecture in Britain had reached a very high level of culture—witness the great minsters, like Lincoln and York, or the great castles, like Windsor and Hampton Court.

Without an elementary knowledge of the English vernacular, no one can fully understand the early English architecture of Virginia. Besides, contrary to popular belief up to this very day, Virginia architecture was much more English than has been supposed.

The Britain of 1600 was a country of fortified manors, battlemented castles, thatched and wattled farmhouses, picturesque chimneystacks, half-timber work, winding tower staircases, and tracery-windowed abbeys, minsters, and little parish churches. For the most part the spirit of this building work was informal, romantic, and naïve; it partook of things not according to rule; it breathed Chaucer.

In short, Britain at that period was a land where *medieval architecture* flourished almost everywhere.

Now what is this Medieval Style which lasted in England more than a thousand years? It comprises three chief divisions: Anglo-Saxon, Norman, and Gothic. Yet the great English Gothic Style is itself subdivided into styles based on window tracery which are called "Early English," "Decorated," "Perpendicular," and "Tudor." Of main concern to us in this essay is that last subdivision, the "Tudor,"—also called "Late Gothic" or "Late Medieval",—which was chiefly centered around the Court of King Henry VIII (1509-1547). It may be necessary to remind the reader that Henry, wife-lover and neck-chopper, was an enthusiastic builder, who initiated in England a domestic architecture in which the desire for comfort was paramount. No better homes have been built in England than at the height of Tudor influence.

Most authorities date medieval architecture as terminating in England in 1558 with the accession of Elizabeth to the throne. But it was not as simple as that. On the contrary, the vast majority of British buildings after 1558 continued to be built in the Tudor or Late Medieval manner, even as late as Queen Anne and the year 1702 or thereabouts. It was this long and widespread persistence of the traditional manner of building which greatly influenced Virginia architecture in the seventeenth century.

Furthermore, there came upon the English scene in Elizabeth's time, an architecture called "Early Renaissance," comprising two styles, the Elizabethan (1558-1603) and the Jacobean (1603-1625). The "Early Renaissance" was followed by the "High Renaissance" in architecture, a subject which has little to do with this essay, but which has much to do with Williamsburg.

But in spite of the penetrating wedge of the "Early Renaissance" into the great mass of English medieval construction, Britain remained a place where medieval building traditions, especially in the rural areas, remained powerful and overwhelmingly popular throughout the seventeenth century. The situation was, for all purposes, like a grain of Renaissance sand in a medieval bucket. *That* we should remember when we survey the early architecture of Virginia.

The significant aspect of the transposition of the English Medieval Style to Virginia was that the "lag"—meaning the delay caused at that period by an architectural style crossing an ocean—served only to bring Virginia closer to the heart of medievalism. This lag in fact gave a new lease on life to the Medieval Style flourishing within the Old Dominion.

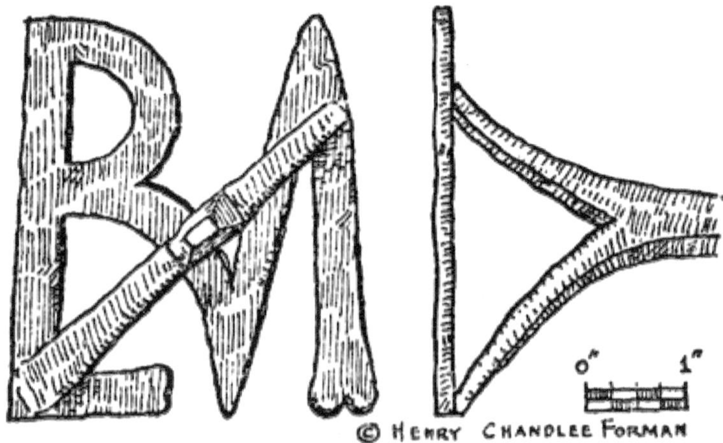

A BRANDING IRON FROM JAMESTOWN.

This implement for marking cattle or hogsheads with the initials R L N came to light in the ruins of the First State House. On the right is shown the side view, with most of the twelve-inch handle excluded.

III

THE ENGLISH STYLES OF ARCHITECTURE IN VIRGINIA

For many years after the founding of James Fort in Virginia, the Indian continued to build in his traditional manner along side the newly-blossoming English architecture. In what year the last, authentic, wooden structure of Indian style was constructed in Virginia by a native Indian is not known, but it probably was in the first quarter of the nineteenth century. However that may be, in eighteenth-century Virginia Indian construction was a dying art, of which the skills, it seems, have been completely lost. Even if you gave the present-day Indians in the Old Dominion the tools to build them with, those natives would not know how to erect the great wigwams and temples of their ancestors. Such a statement is no minimization, because this writer once resided as a guest in the Pamunkey Indian Reservation near West Point, Virginia, and he found the natives there, who are descendants of the oldest and most powerful clan in Virginia, who possess the oldest Indian reservation in the United States, living in clapboard houses of the kind we call "shacks." With all their inherited courtly bearing and good manners, they had even forgotten how to make their own pottery, with its indigenous designs based on the scroll, the swastika, and the like. Instead, they sold to tourists and visitors to the reservation imported Southwestern or Pueblo pottery, of step-designs. To that favor they had come at last, three centuries after Jamestown.

The fact that a large percent of the people who settled Jamestown, and other English settlements of Virginia in the seventeenth century were lowly fishermen, farmers and laborers who were not adjusted to new national economic conditions, unsuccessful tradesmen, unemployed craftsmen, and such folk, has a direct bearing on the style of architecture introduced from Britain into Virginia. Because there were few bluebloods, and because most were of the humbler classes, the average Virginian came from the overwrought farms on remote and secluded roads, the little small-town shops, in narrow streets, the peasant dwellings of sod or wattle, far out on the fens and moors of Britain. The real point is, architecturally speaking, it was in these very rural districts of England the Medieval Style was the most entrenched.

It can not be said that the yeomen, the sawyers, the joiners, the hog-raisers, the merchants, or the carpenters of Jamestown Island—and we know many by name and exactly where they lived there—were interested in the continental, classical or Renaissance ideas in architecture which were commencing to be fashionable among the rich and affluent. It was, on the contrary, those very same poorer classes, ill-affording and not understanding the Renaissance fads, who were the most reactionary of all in their approach to building methods. They loved medieval architecture. They doted on their Gothic heritage, whether it were a diamond-pane casement or a stock floor plan for a traditional house.

By the year 1615—eight years after the founding of James Fort—the great English architect, Inigo Jones, had taken home from Italy a number of books by Palladio, distinguished Italian architect in the classical manner, and by 1622 had completed the important banqueting hall at "White Hall," London, replete with rows of classical pilasters. But the Virginia settlers—probably at least ninety-five percent of them — knew nothing of Inigo Jones and Palladio, because, in their arts and crafts thinking, the colonists were overwhelmingly medieval.

We come, now, to the three English styles of architecture prevalent in Virginia in the seventeenth century: the Medieval, the Jacobean, and the Transitional. The first two were common throughout that hundred years, but the third, the Transitional, began about 1680 and extended about one-third of the way into the eighteenth century.

I. THE MEDIEVAL STYLE

The buildings represented by this first style should be spoken of as "Virginia Medieval Architecture," because that is what the style is. "Colonial" and "Early Colonial" are technically not correct names for the style. This particular manifestation in architecture belonged to the style, English Medieval; it was the direct product, not an "afterglow," of the Middle Ages.

The Old Dominion at this time was full of medieval structures, of which there were hundreds of kinds of every description: windmills, water mills, taverns, guest houses, coffee houses, churches, mansions, dwellings, hovels, state houses, glebes, brew-houses, warehouses, furnaces, stores, shops, tanneries, market houses, guard houses, blockhouses, tenements, silk factories, and countless outhouses. Taken as a whole, these buildings possessed Tudor features identical to those which we find in the medieval architecture of Britain: steeply-pointed roofs, half-timber work, the huge "pyramid" chimney, "black-diapered" brickwork patterns of glazed brick, and casements on hinges. Others are: separate or grouped chimney stacks, overhanging storeys, beamed ceilings, buttresses, stair towers, and "outshuts" — wart-like additions. These are a few of the Tudor motifs; there are many more. Generally the overall building designs were marked by informality and naïveté. Some of these medieval Virginia buildings, such as the "Thorough-good House" (c. 1640), and the "One-Bay Dwelling" (c. 1670), of which we present several illustrations, are still extant.

II. THE JACOBEAN STYLE

Although only a little wedge at first, when it came upon the English scene, the Early Renaissance Style of architecture slowly and gradually developed and expanded. As we have noted, it combined two phases, first the Elizabethan Style, and then the Jacobean, much of which was based either directly or indirectly upon Dutch, Flemish, and German architecture. On the other hand, in Virginia these two styles, Elizabethan and Jacobean, are for practical purposes combined into one style, called "Jacobean."

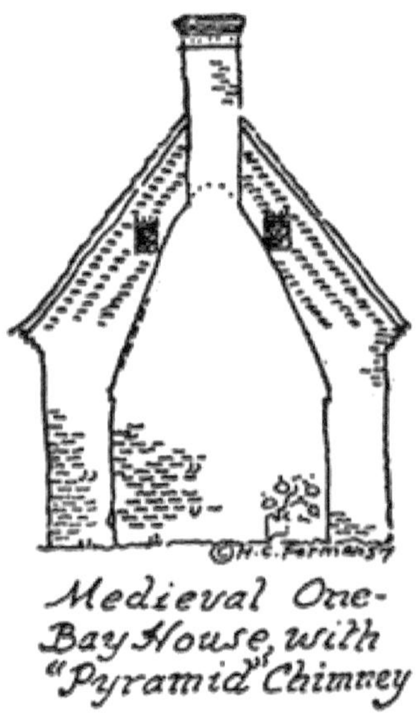

Medieval One-Bay House, with "Pyramid" Chimney

A Jacobean Church in Virginia · Author's Restoration ·

At the same time, this Virginia Jacobean was never an important and wide-spread manner of building. To all intents and purposes it was a minor style, domi-nated by, or grafted upon, the Medieval Style. You may think of it as a kind of win-dow dressing upon the Medieval. Its chief example extant in the Old Dominion is "Bacon's Castle" (c. 1650), in Surry County.

For the most part you may recognize the Jacobean by Cupid's bow lines in house gables, door heads, window heads, and stair balusters. Such lines reveal the decorative and exuberant curves loved much by the Low Countrymen and by the Englishmen who took over the curves. All in all, Virginia saw relatively little of the Jacobean because it was a minor style.

III. THE TRANSITIONAL STYLE

More complicated than either of the first two styles is the Transitional—an architectural style identified and named by this writer to include all experimental examples which formed the transitional link between the Medieval of the seventeenth century and the Georgian of the eighteenth. This style of the Transition prevailed in England, but as far as we know has not been identified or labelled as such.

It seems that in the last quarter of the seventeenth century, that is, from about 1680, Virginians generally were becoming weary of their dark medieval cottages, mostly one room in depth, with a loft above, and with the only daylight entering through small casements of opaque glass. These people began to look toward a goal which may have been vaguely defined in their minds: a handsome and ship-shape residence, preferably of brick, of two rooms deep and two storeys-and-garret high, with wings or separate dependencies to balance; a neat and orderly mansion, without steep gables, but with one cornice line for the whole building. This goal, of course, was the Georgian mansion of the eighteenth century.

At any rate, between 1680 and 1730 change permeated the air of Virginia, and a whole host of experimental buildings sprang up which we loosely label as "Transitional."

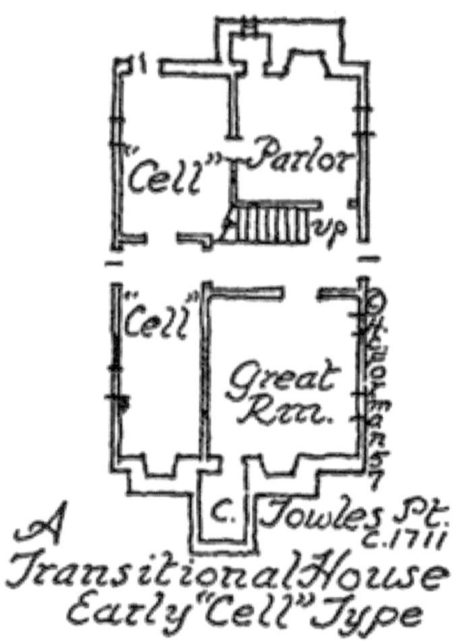

In the first place, the sash or "guillotine" window is one of the barometers indicating the Transitional stage to Georgian. No doubt by the 1680s such windows, comprising crude, vertically-sliding sash, which often fell suddenly on wrist or neck, like a French *guillotine*, were introduced into Virginia. But not until 1699 do the records reveal their existence, at which time they were specified for the Capitol in Williamsburg. Notwithstanding, such sash before 1700 was a rarity, because the casement window was still fashionable.

Other first signs of the Transition are the diagonal or catercornered fireplace, the hipped or "pyramid" roof, the gambrel roof, and the open-well stairs, which mount up the sides of a room—an arrangement which Britons at home complained of as "wasters of space." In short, it may be said that while these features may earmark a building as of the Transition, they are only thus *when* combined with certain house-forms and floor plans. A diagonal fireplace by itself is no criterion of a building being Transitional.

Many of the dwellings of this Style were "cell" houses. That is, there was a "cell" or "aisle" at the rear of the narrow Tudor cottage, one room deep. In the same way, the English parish church of single nave sometimes sprouted a side aisle in order to make more space for parishioners. In the Old Dominion such elongated warts or "outshuts" at the rear of the homestead afforded additional bedroom space over and beyond the cramped garret, but at the same time unfortunately threw off-center the steep medieval gable, thereby causing what the English have called a "catslide." A catslide roof is one in which the slope at the rear extends nearly the whole way to the ground. In New England the "cell" addition became the "lean-to." For such fabrics in Virginia we have coined the term, the *Early Cell* type, one which was well represented by the destroyed "Towles Point," in Lancaster County.

Even so, the Virginian did not long relish an "ugly," though perhaps picturesque, catslide gable; therefore, he once more began to build symmetrically, at the same time keeping his little back "cells." When such gables became symmetrical, we may assign the examples to the *Late Cell* type.

We find, moreover, that not all Transitional structures had "cells." Sometimes the mark of experimentation is shown by other building forms, such as the one-room deep cottage mushrooming upward into a full second storey and garret; at other times the settler, dissatisfied with his "knock-head" bed chambers, experimented with the gambrel roof, frequently but mistakenly called the "Dutch roof." The gambrel, to the best of our knowledge, was introduced from England into the American Colonies in the 1680s; but it did not become widespread for almost half a century. Likewise Transitional are certain early Virginia homes with hip roofs, perhaps the best example being the brick "Abingdon Glebe" (c. 1700) in Gloucester

County, where the one-and-a-half-storey main block of the house is exactly balanced by low end pavilions—each surmounted by a hipped roof.

There were other Virginia building experiments in the period covered by the Transition, but the foregoing is sufficient to summarize the Style, which paved the way for the Georgian in the eighteenth century.

IV

THE DEVELOPMENT OF ENGLISH ARCHITEC-
TURE IN VIRGINIA.

I. THE COTTAGE PERIOD

The thirteen years between the founding of James Fort in 1607 and the landing of the Pilgrim Fathers at Plymouth Rock on Christmas Day, 1620, have been designated by this writer, for the sake of convenience, as the "Cottage" Period of Virginia architecture. It was in the "Cradle of the Republic," on James River, that we find the English styles taking root and flourishing mightily. As a result, the United States of America became characterized more by these same English styles than by any other foreign style, such as French or Spanish.

For the most part—though not entirely—these first thirteen years of English settlement in Virginia were marked by rough shelters, temporary huts or booths, and fragile buildings. As a case in point, the first fortification thrown together upon the day of first landing upon Jamestown Island was of the skimpiest construction: boughs of trees cast together in the form of a half-moon. The first settlement at that time was frankly a bivouac, where a tented church was set up, and the customary lodging was a tent cover or a hole in the ground. Secretary Strachey wrote home to England about the ill-lodged colonists, of whom the poorer slept on the ground and the more fortunate had such miserable cottages that the sun pierced through them and made them hot as stoves.

All these fragile shelters have disappeared, but types of them have in later years been described. In 1621, for example, a servant by the name of Richard Chelsey was to have a new house built for him, in length, fourteen feet, and in breadth, twelve feet. In Northampton County one John Alford squeezed himself into a hut only five and a half feet high, with a doorway only four feet, nine inches and a quarter in height. Big enough for children! Some habitations did not bother about wood for walls; they were of earth or clay mixed with straw. This last type was represented in later years by some of the outhouses at "Four Mile Tree" plantation, Virginia, which were made of red clay held together by chopped straw.

Such abbreviated buildings had waxed paper or curtains to cover their "windholes," sliding-panel windows, hinged shutters without glass, or tiny casements.

In addition to these frail and temporary shelters were more substantial edifices, which may be classified, according to present knowledge, as illustrating at least five chief methods of English Medieval construction. These may be listed as follows:

1. The palisade
2. The puncheon
3. The cruck
4. Timber framing, including half-timber work
5. Brick

Now the first of these, *palisading*, was common in England for two thousand years and more, and, as we have already seen, was employed by the Virginia Indian, who invented it entirely independently of European contact. The first palisade on the James River, that of James Fort of 1607, comprised strong planks and posts placed close together four feet deep in the earth. They rose above ground about fourteen feet. But there was nothing, to our knowledge, which was unusual about that palisading, except, perhaps, its triangular shape. Most forts of that kind were square, but on Jamestown Island the fort was a triangle, supposedly forced into that configuration by the topography. At any rate, the customary bulwarks or watchtowers rose at the three corners of the fortification, and there was the usual moat and drawbridge.

English forts of this kind, with stockades and ditches, were common to Virginia, as for example, at Sir Walter Raleigh's Roanoke Fort of 1585 in North Carolina, formerly Virginia; at Old Point Comfort in 1609; in City of Henrico in 1611; at Claiborne's Kent Island trading post of 1621—now in Maryland; and at the "Town" on the Eastern Shore in 1623. One of the longest palisades in all Virginia in the seventeenth century was Dale's "Dutch Gap" on the James. Its two-mile-long moat was lined by palisaded walls accented by towers.

After the Massacre of 1622, the Colony of Virginia ordered (1624-25) all dwellings and plantations to be palisaded in, that is, to be enclosed by "Park-pales," as the English called them. Ordinarily walls about seven and a half feet high were tall enough for protection from sudden attack. Even churches were palisaded in, as for example, the first church on the Eastern shore. In the 1630s one Stephen Charleton threatened to kick the Reverend Cotton over the paled fence—the "Pallyzados"—around that sacred edifice.

The second medieval method is *puncheoning*. It seems that the English made puncheons or "quarters" pretty much like the Indians, that is, they fashioned upright timbers or posts, set apart in the ground so that the space between them was the same as the thickness of the timber or post. Then they filled the interstices with "wattle-and-daub," a basketwork of branches, twigs, and roots, coated on both sides with loam and lime, mixed with straw. Back home in England, this filling of the spaces was named "post and pan." On James River there is record of the Berkeley settlement of 1619 having most of the dwellings built of "punches" set in the earth and with boards for the roofs. Other huts were flimsy shelters merely "covered with boards," so that one spark could easily set them off. But when the English employed thin turf or sod for their roofs, the structures were safer from fire.

In connection with this wattling and daubing of Virginia buildings, the two early churches on Eastern Shore are believed to have been puncheoned edifices. The second church (c. 1638), near Fishing Creek was described as "of insignificant dimensions" and constructed of two materials: "roughly riled logs"—that is, vertical timbers, since log cabins as we know them were virtually unknown in the English colonies before 1660; and "wattles." A reference to "daubing" the first church (c. 1623), on King's Creek, leads us to believe that it also was built on "punches" and was woven with wattles.

Now, about the third construction type, the *cruck*. No one has seen today an original cruck building in this country, but early Virginia possessed hundreds and perhaps thousands of cruck fabrics. Like the palisade and puncheon methods, the cruck was medieval down to its very core. In describing the James Fort church of 1607, Captain John Smith stated it was set upon "crotchets," covered with rafters, rushes, and earth. When he spoke of crotchet, he probably meant cruck, of which it was a later derivative. At all events, a building set on crucks means that it is supported or hung upon pairs of curved or bent tree trunks placed together in the shape of a Gothic pointed arch and spaced one "bay" apart. It was the custom in medieval England to erect buildings in bays for the sake of convenience. A bay was the standard unit of length, generally sixteen feet, although it could vary. A four-bay cruck church on Jamestown Island means that there were five pairs of bent trees, or crucks, in total length some sixty-four feet, arranged in the following manner: : : : : : Then, upon the crucks were hung the side walls and the roof.

Yet in this era of Virginia history before the "Mayflower" landed in New England, the most common of all the medieval types of construction is *timber-framing*. A building which was timber-framed was a substantial one, comprising a framework of posts set *far* apart, of diagonal braces, and of studs, sills, plates, and girts — the ensemble fastened together securely with tongues and grooves and wooden pegs. It was the custom to cut and adz the timbers so that they would fit together neatly; and in order to do that, Roman numerals were cut into each timber to identify it. In that way the whole framework could be assembled properly and efficiently — the first pre-fabricated house in Virginia. So good were these timber-framed structures that the English in the Old Dominion called them "fair houses" and "English houses." In 1611 James City boasted of two fair rows of dwellings, all of framed timber, two storeys and garret, or corn-loft, high. At Berkeley, in 1619 there were two timber-framed habitations, and at the City of Henrico in 1611 three streets of well framed houses.

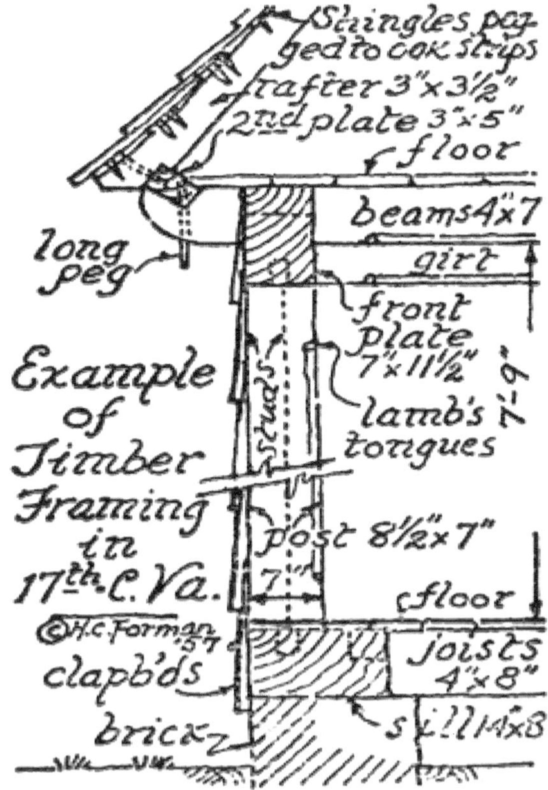

The timber-framed dwelling is the most commonly erected today in this country, although builders and carpenters no longer bother to number or to peg together the timbers.

In this Cottage Period about which we have been reading the general manner of framing structures was to either cover the framework or make "half-timber work." In the former method, weatherboarding (clapboards), or shingle tiles or slate nailed to weatherboards, covered up the posts and studs. In the latter method, the filling between the studding would be left exposed to the elements. And this filling could take a variety of forms: plaster; "wattle-and-daub"; brick "nogging," with the bricks laid horizontally, in herring-bone, or helter-skelter; or mud and straw.

Contrary to popular opinion, there were undoubtedly *brick* buildings in Virginia in the first thirteen years. It was at Jamestown in 1607 that President Wingfield visited "ould Short, the bricklayer." What do you suppose Short did in those early years of the Colony? He manufactured brick for chimneys, walks, walls, terraces, floors, kilns, and buildings—*brick* buildings. Now brick for an edifice, usually laid in English bond, where the courses are alternately headers and stretchers, is still another English medieval method of construction, which became popular in Virginia. We know, for instance, that there were in 1611, in addition to the well-framed dwellings already cited at City of Henrico, some "competent and decent houses, the first storie all of brick." These were not purely brick structures but only part brick, which we have called buildings of "half-and-half work." The downstairs was brick, the upstairs timber-framed—another English medieval type.

Further, during the Cottage Period and for many a year afterward, the wooden chimney was the common method of smoke outlet. Strachey mentioned at James City not only the wattled buildings, but the "wide and large Country chimnies"—in other words, the wood or "Welsh" chimney, a medieval construction which dates back in English history to the eleventh century and before. Ordinarily the fire had its smoke and sparks sucked up a large wattle-and-daubed or lath-and-plastered hood resting on the garret floor, thence up a wood flue and out the stack, which might have been a barrel or wood box or some such contraption. At other times the whole chimney and fireplace were placed on the exterior, the better to protect against fire; and the boards were lined with crude lath and clay daubing. Still another kind of chimney was the "catted" chimney, made of "cats" or rolled-up strips of clay mixed with straw, and placed closely together within a framework of wooden posts and rails. But you have to see these wooden chimneys to know how they actually appeared.

＊ ＊ ＊ ＊ ＊

The story of this thirteen year period from 1607 to 1620 should not be concluded without mention of the influence of Indian building methods upon the English settlers. In 1608, after the great smoke of the fire had blown away from James City, the colonists under the direction of Captain Newport roofed some of their new homes with the bark of trees, which was cooler than their usual roofing clapboards or wooden shingles. Also they adorned their new rooms with mats woven into delicate colors and designs by the Indians.

Thatch for roofs did not go out of style altogether in favor of bark, because as late as 1638 there is record of a "thatcht" dwelling on the Eastern Shore of Virginia.

Plowden noted the construction in 1650 in some of our East Coast settlements of "arbour" houses, of poles and bark boards; and some of these *English* arbor buildings were undoubtedly built in Jamestown and the other major settlements in earliest Virginia.

While the white man sometimes copied the Indian in his construction, it is significant that when the colonists landed in 1607, the Indian, for his part, was already employing several types of English medieval construction, which he had invented and acquired independently of European contact. Although we have already cited most of these types, we list them again, in order to give the Indian credit, where credit is due: palisaded walls with moats, and pale fencing; puncheoning with wattles; central hearths with roof louvres for smoke; thatched roofs; and timber-framing with wattle-and-daub panels. How can anyone belittle the technical accomplishments of the Indian by calling him "savage," when in at least five building methods he equalled the white man bringing the English Medieval Style to these shores? Our English ancestors *originally* lived in smoky buildings with the central open hearth in the middle of the great room; in seventeenth-century Virginia the Indian did likewise. The difference was in timing.

II. THE COUNTRY HOUSE

In the seventeenth century, the English rural homestead was usually placed along the great Bay, the Chesapeake, or upon one of its tidewater tributaries. Back of such a seat, or on either side of it, there stretched the outhouses, generally arranged in rows or around courtyards. The water served as the principal highway, and the plantation depended upon it. Certain Indian paths, it is true, were turned into narrow lanes for carts, in order to reach the interior, like the oldest "road" in Virginia, which, as we have seen, extended from Jamestown to Middle Plantation, now Williamsburg.

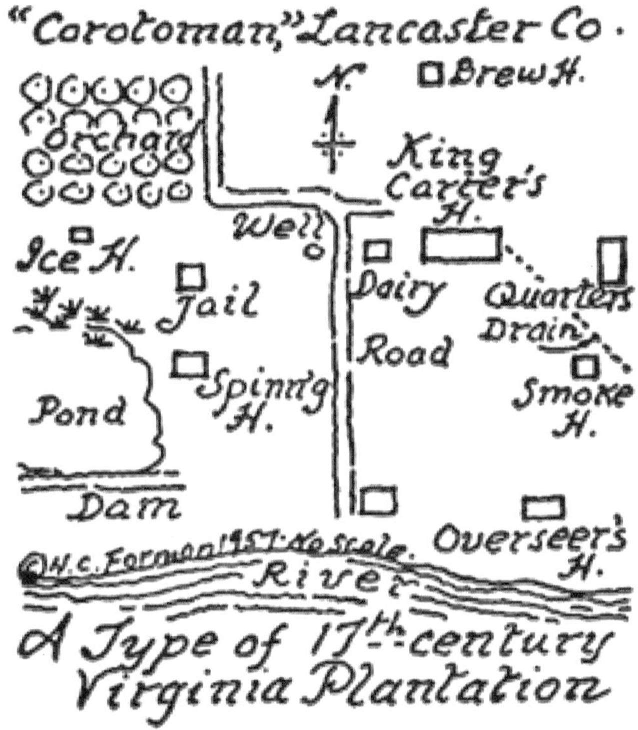

The variety and number of properties which the prosperous land-owners possessed is revealing, by giving us a glimpse of the economic and architectural life of the times. Besides the mansion-house there were offices, kitchens and bake houses, slave quarters, school houses, dairies, barns, stables, granaries, smoke houses, spring houses, and dovecots.

There were servants' dwellings, spinning houses, smithies, tan houses, bin houses, well houses, hogsties, cornhouses, and guest houses. For the gardens, sometimes called "hortyards," there were summerhouses, greenhouses, and arbors. Then there were bloomeries and ironworks, wharves for landing goods, called "bridges," warehouses, windmills, watermills, sawmills, glassworks, silkhouses, brick and pottery kilns, lime kilns, saltworks, and blockhouses.

For all intents and purposes such grandiose estates were self-sustaining. Those goods not produced in Virginia came generally from England and were usually landed upon the wharf in front of the plantation-dwelling. That the kitchen outhouse was frequently placed at a distance from the dining room was primarily due not to class or color distinction, but to the medieval custom of carrying food across the service courtyard.

Very often throughout the seventeenth century, especially on the Eastern Shore of Virginia, the kitchen building was tied to the main abode by a colonnade—a passage with columns—or by a curtain—a covered passageway.

That these edifices in their wooden parts were painted, when the owner could afford paint, is proven by the record of importations of large quantities of color pigments and oils to make paint. Many of us today think that the early Virginia building was white, but colors like gray and tan were common. When the owner could not bear the expense of painting, he left his house bare or "whited" it with good white lime—that is, used whitewash.

SOME OCCUPANTS OF 17TH-CENTURY VIRGINIA HOMES ATE FROM BOWLS LIKE THIS ONE, FROM JAMESTOWN

A scraffito or scratched slipware bowl with one handle. Height $3\frac{5}{8}$", dia. $8\frac{3}{4}$". *Photo, author.* (See page 17)

A MEDIEVAL "PYRAMID" CHIMNEY IN VIRGINIA

So large is the fireplace of this one-bay dwelling that you can burn an eight-foot log within it. Great "weatherings" taper the chimney towards the stack, which is freestanding as protection against fire. Note medieval "black-diapered" brick pattern in gable. *Photo, author.* (See page 19)

REMNANTS OF A MEDIEVAL VIRGINIA STOREHOUSE

The foundation of the "Bin House," Jamestown, excavated by the National Park Service. The two brick bins have concave floors below the original main floor level. *Photo, author.* (See page 32)

A TYPE OF MEDIEVAL CORNICE IN VIRGINIA

Unlike the later box cornice, to which we are accustomed, the cornice of this dwelling of about 1670 has exposed and rounded beam ends, which are pegged to a tilted plate, on which the rafters rest. Note corbel of overlapping bricks which stops cornice. *Photo, author.* (See page 42)

A MEDIEVAL "HALL-AND-PARLOR" HOUSE IN JAMES CITY COUNTY

The "Warburton House" or "Pinewoods" of about 1680 has segmental-arched openings, "T"-chimneys, and chimney caps with mouse-tooth brickwork, a decoration which seems to have come into fashion about that time. A rear wing has disappeared. *Photo, author.* (See page 44)

"SWEET HALL," A MEDIEVAL "T"-PLAN HOME IN VIRGINIA

This old seat of the Claibornes in King William County, dating from about 1695, has very tall "T"-stacks, with "weatherings" or slopes above the ridge, and with heavy, ornate caps. The dormers and porches are later. *Photo, author.* (See page 45)

CLAY ROOFING PANTILES FROM THE FIRST STATE HOUSE, JAMESTOWN

The left-hand tile, nearly complete, has a "nob" at one end to catch on the roof strips. It was pieced together by Mr. John T. Zaharov, and is the *first* pantile ever found in the United States. The paper arrow at right marks cemented overlap. *Photo, author.* (See page 48)

ONE OF THE MOST HISTORIC SITES IN THE UNITED STATES

Much of our knowledge of 17th-century Virginia life and art comes from Jamestown foundations. This interesting "complex" of ruins reveals William Sherwood's house cellar of c. 1677-80, and in the immediate foreground, a fireplace hearth of the "Governor's House," probably built in the 1620s, and occupied by Sir George Yeardley. *Photo, author.* (see page 53)

A JAMESTOWN LATTICE CASEMENT AS IT CAME FROM THE GROUND

This medieval window, with the diamond panes or "quarrels" knocked out, came from the "Double House on the Land of Thomas Hampton," and is drawn restored in *Jamestown and St. Mary's*. Note pane of glass standing upon a Dutch brick. *Photo, author.* (See page 68)

TWO UNUSUAL JAMESTOWN STRAP-HINGES

The right-hand hinge, broken, probably came from a wagon-box or chest. (See page 69)

A BRASS SWORD HANDLE FROM THE JAMESTOWN MUD

Found in three pieces with the blade missing, this cavalier's sword is ornamented with *putti* and other decorations. *Photos, author. Courtesy, Antiques Magazine.*

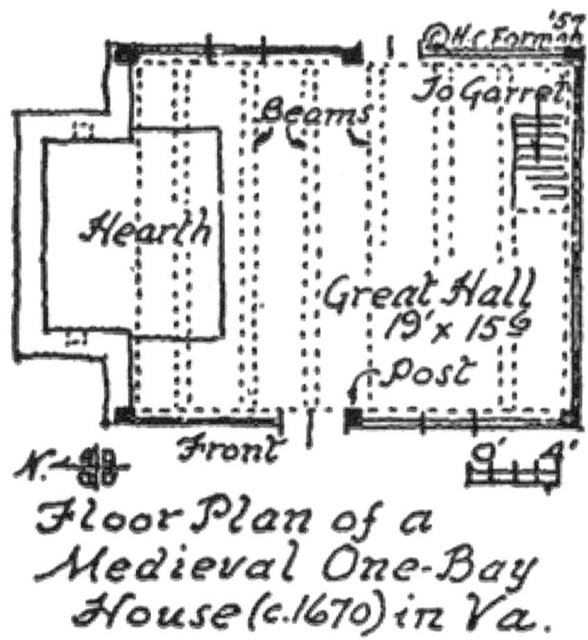

The most significant aspect of the medieval rural abode in Virginia was its regular course of development from the simple, one-room-and-garret cottage—what an English bishop in 1610 called a "silly cote," a hut of "one bay's breath"—to the stately and elegant Georgian mansion of the eighteenth century. Even so, it may not be unequivocally declared that all the simple dwellings were constructed first and all the complex ones later. At the same time, we find that often the homes with more than two downstairs rooms and a central passageway were constructed in late seventeenth-century times. Further, the country lodging for the most part was only one-storey-and-loft high. The full two-storey domicile was the exception.

The elementary hut of one bay, such as we have noted as having been prevalent in the Cottage Period of the first thirteen years, was the earliest type of substantial house-form in the Old Dominion; it had a "hall," which was the "Great Room"—not a passage,—a dining room, and a kitchen, all rolled into one. The garret with sloping ceilings, perhaps reached by a stepladder or narrow, winding, "break-your-neck" staircase, was usually a cold, unheated, cramped space for sleeping.

One of these small, fractional-bay dwellings stood (1660) in Northampton County, and was ten feet from end to end. It served as the first meeting-place of the Quakers or Friends on the Eastern Shore, and was later used as a "wheat house."

A better known one-bay domicile was Richard May's, built about 1661 in Jamestown, and pictured in a crude sort of way in the Ambler Manuscripts: a flush chimney at one gable and a front with central door flanked on each side by a window. Excavations by the National Park Service at the site of May's revealed that the house had a chimney at the opposite end—a feature which must of necessity have marked an addition.

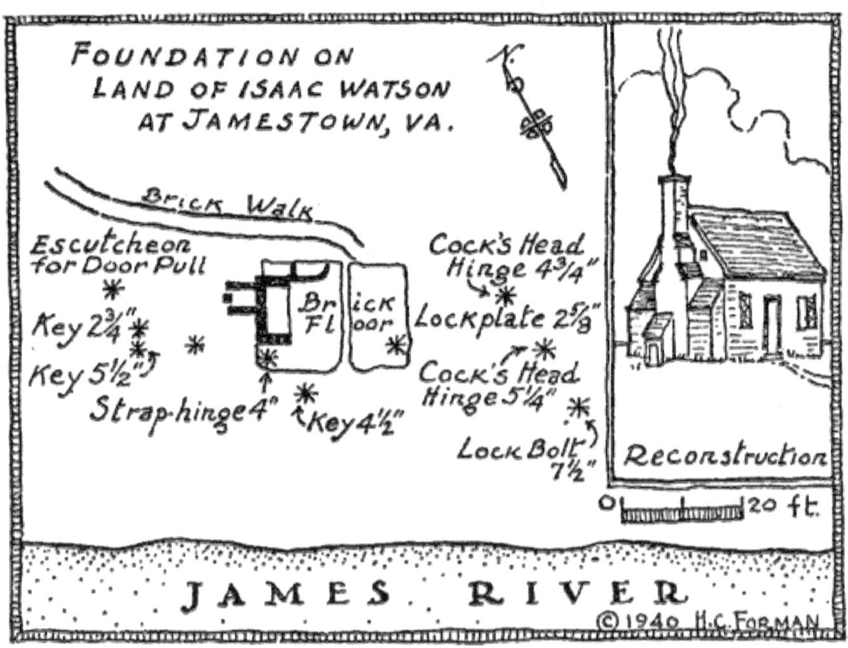

PLAN OF A HOUSE-FOUNDATION ON THE LAND OF ISAAC WATSON AT JAMESTOWN.

Showing the distribution of important hardware, and a reconstruction of the house. *Courtesy Antiques Magazine.*

One of the few known ruins of a one-bay dwelling was excavated at Jamestown under this writer's direction and was designated as the timber-framed "House on Isaac Watson's Land," built possibly as early as 1644. Before its destruction, it comprised one "hall," twenty feet by twenty, with a great projecting fireplace at one gable big enough for an eight-foot log to burn. The chimney must have been what we call a "pyramid," and it was flanked on either side by small "outshuts," which were probably "ingle recesses" or "chimney-pents." Inside, there was a Dutch oven at one side of the fireplace and a setting for a brewing copper next to it. This was no pauper's hovel, for the casements were leaded, and the hardware included fancy wrought-iron hinges, including the fairly-rare "Cock's Head" hinge.

Another structure of this type is here illustrated under the caption, "Medieval One-Bay House" (c. 1670) in Virginia. Without including its tremendous "pyramid" chimney, the dwelling measures twenty-and-a-half feet long and sixteen wide. The chimney end is wholly brick, and the other three sides clapboarded. The one downstairs room, the "Great Hall," has exposed posts, beams, and wall plates, with chamfers terminating in crude "lamb's tongues." In a corner opposite the fireplace there was a stepladder or very steep staircase, only twenty-seven inches wide. Upstairs there was one sleeping room with two tiny, lie-on-your-stomach windows—almost peep-holes—to give air and light. There were no dormers, and the long cedar shingles were pegged to thin oaken strips across the rafters. Even the floor beams were pegged to the rafters so that the roof on a stormy night would not part company with the "Great Hall."

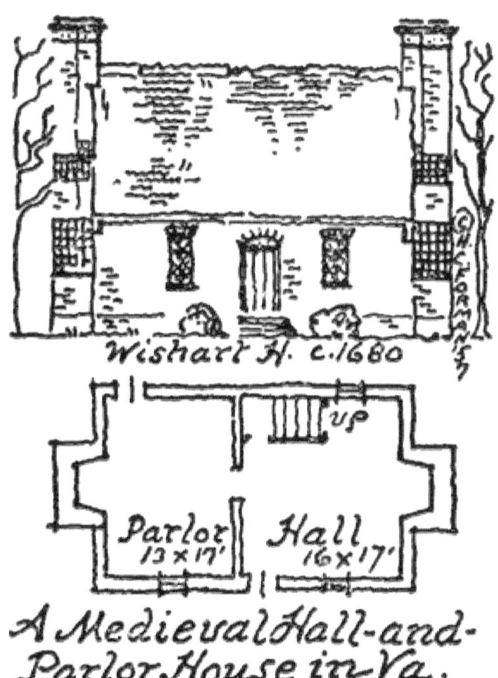

A Medieval Hall-and-Parlor House in Va.

When the planter or tradesman became a little wealthier, or his family became larger, it was a simple matter to add a "parlor" to one end of the homestead, thus making the second stage of development, the "hall-and-parlor" dwelling. There was a regular "school" of building of such habitations in seventeenth-century Virginia. In such examples the parlor was smaller than the "Hall" or "Great Room." Sometimes, of course, the early settler commenced with a "hall-and-parlor" residence built all at once.

The foremost example of this type in the Old Dominion is the "Adam Thoroughgood House" (c. 1640), Princess Anne County, a brick storey-and-garret dwelling, with a flush chimney at one gable and a "pyramid" at the other. The chimney-stacks are "T"s, meaning that they are designed in that shape in plan to reveal multiple flues. The brickwork is English bond, and the windows, before alterations, were leaded casements. The doors, too, were battened, or built up with boards. All the openings have segmental arches, and high up on the brick gables are lines of glazed header bricks parallel to the rakes.

Of the same ilk is another brick lodging, the "Wishart House" (c. 1680) in Norfolk, which has two pyramid, "T"-chimneys, and a cornice terminated by little corbels of overlapping brick—a common medieval feature. Other extant examples are "Sweet Hall" (c. 1695) and "Warburton House" (c. 1680), both of which had a projecting addition at the rear. In fact the records are full of "hall-and-parlor" houses which may have been destroyed, such as Sam Wools' plantation (1638) on Eastern Shore, twenty-five feet long and sixteen wide—a standard size. There was "one partition in it," and it had only one chimney and only one wing, a buttery. The kitchen, it seems, was not mentioned, but it probably was an outhouse.

It was a natural step to the third development, the "central-passage" type, a group of buildings named by this writer for the purpose of convenience. A "screen" or wooden partition was added to the end of the "Hall" or Great Room in order to make a passage from front to back in the center of the edifice. In that way the living space, the "Hall," was made more private than when it served as a passageway. At any rate, the brick "Keeling House" (c. 1700), Princess Anne County, is a good specimen. A later, or "Hangover" phase of the central-passage type is "Smith's Fort Plantation," generally known as the "Rolfe House," Surry County, which has been continuously and erroneously dated 1652, but which really belongs to the first half of the eighteenth century.

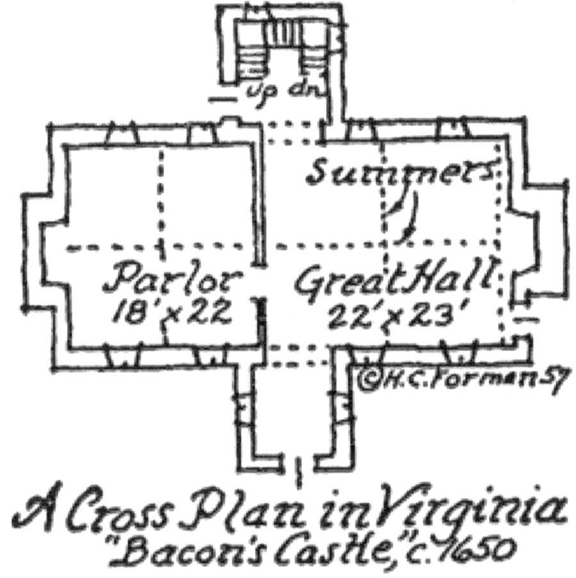

A Cross Plan in Virginia
"Bacon's Castle," c. 1650

The last or culminating development in the rural dwelling was the changing of a "hall-and-parlor" habitation, or one of "central-passage" variety, into a "cross-house." The cross was formed by adding an enclosed porch, usually with a "porch chamber" above it, on the front façade, and a wing, like a stair tower, to the rear. However, a "T"-shaped domicile, with no back wing, is also classified as a "cross-house." An old record tells of one Southey Littleton, of Accomack, who had a porch and porch chamber on the front of his dwelling—in other words, a cross-house. Of the extant or partially extant examples in Virginia are "Bacon's Castle" (c. 1650), Surry County; "Malvern Hill" (c. 1662), Henrico County; and "Christ's Cross" (c. 1690) and "Foster's Castle," (c. 1685) both in New Kent. They make a veritable school of building which once must have flourished the length and breadth of tidewater Virginia. With its noted "Bond Castle," Maryland, too, had a school of cross-houses.

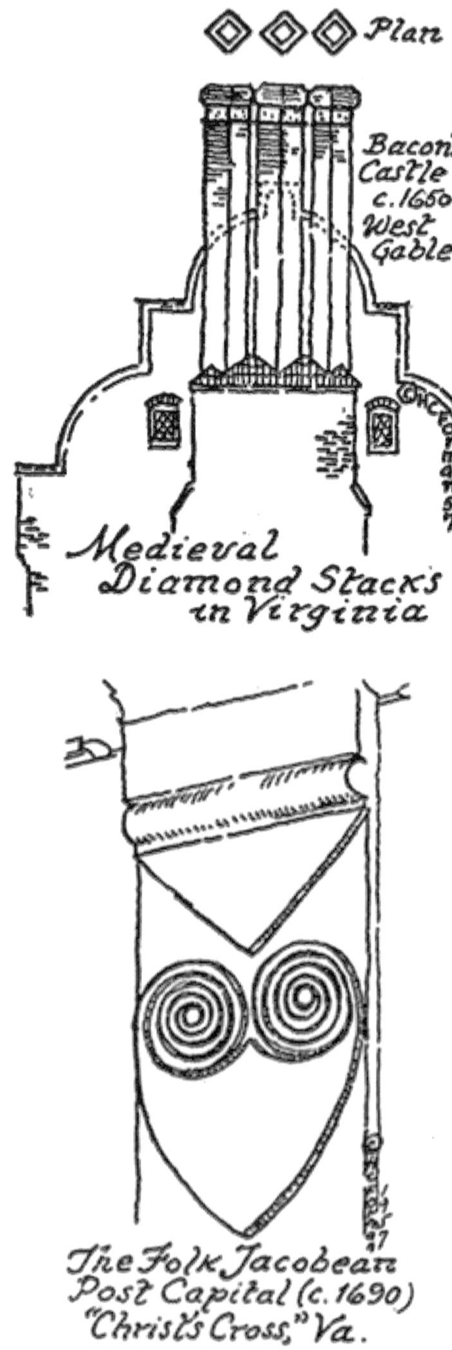

Of the Virginia examples, "Bacon's Castle," two-storeys-and-garret high, with basement, was built by one Arthur Allen, and was named for the rebel, Nathaniel Bacon, who in 1676 ordered his men to capture the dwelling. "Castle" meant "fort." Its cross-plan incorporated a porch, porch chamber, and stair tower. A low, wooden, curtain and kitchen extension, which is believed to have been seventeenth century in date, formerly stood off the gable on the "Hall" side—an arrangement indicating that the Great Room perhaps also served as a dining room. The curtain was the buttery, or bottlery.

But the most distinguishing feature of "Bacon's Castle" is the Jacobean "curvilinear" gable at each end. These gables possess round members—"cuspings"—and steps, built pretty much the same way in which they were made in England and the Low Countries. The chimney stacks are Tudor, three in number, set diagonally on their bases at each gable. Because of the way these chimneys look in plan, we call them "diamond stacks."

Also Jacobean are the crude brick pediment over the main entrance, now much changed, and the brick borders surrounding the windows—called "enframements." And of course, the windows formerly held leaded casements, with mullions and transom bars.

Two important features of another of the cross-houses mentioned belong to "Christ's Cross," called for short, "Criss Cross." This writer can remember when there was hardly a person who knew of the existence of this place, and where it was located. The double door opening out into the enclosed porch from the "Hall" we have denoted as the "finest Tudor door in all Virginia"—because of its panel design and Gothic mouldings; and the post in the "Hall" has probably the finest Jacobean carved capital in the United States. The capital is in truth a *folk* Jacobean carving, a grotesque, comprising a raised heart-shaped shield with crudely chiselled volutes upon it, and an "echinus" or cushion, and an "abacus" or block above it. It reminds one of the ancient Greek Ionic wooden capitals in Athens, Asia Minor, or elsewhere, which possessed rough or incipient volutes.

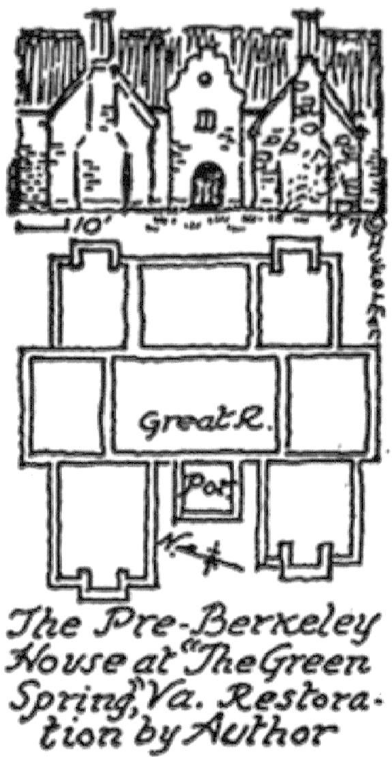

The Pre-Berkeley House at "The Green Spring," Va. Restoration by Author

Study of the cross-house in Virginia needs an essay to itself. We have tried here to give some of the highlights of this last development of the rural dwelling, which is outstandingly medieval in design and construction—with a bit here and there of Jacobean trimming.

Archaic Ionic Cap found at Athens

Branching off the main stream of country house development are exceptions and special cases, such as "The Green Spring" mansion (c. 1646), Sir William Berkeley's home near Jamestown. Sometimes it is mistakenly called the first large country house in America, but it may not lay claim to that status since the earlier "Governor's Castle" in Maryland had a larger area. However that may be, "The

Green Spring" for its time was baronial. It seems to have been a "double-parlor" dwelling—an English derivative, where the "Hall" stood between two parlors. When the recently-revealed watercolor of this mansion-house by Benjamin Henry Latrobe is published, its features, like the roof "shingled" with dormers and the front porch of "clumsy Jacobean brickwork" may be more fully described.

In the recent excavations at "The Green Spring" were found the brick footings of a *pre*-Berkeley building. We know that it antedated Sir William's great pile because part of it was covered by Sir William's structure. Our floor plan, based on Kocher, Waterman, and Dimmick, shows a very unusual room arrangement for seventeenth-century Virginia. It looks very much like an "E"-plan of the Elizabethan Style of architecture. And at the rear were "cells" or "outshuts." With grains of allowance, the sketch of the entrance front is conjectural, but probably has enough of the truth about it to reveal the unique character of the edifice.

III. THE TOWN DWELLING

Because Virginians in founding their towns wished to crowd their houses in rows along their streets, the city abode is substantially different in type from the rural one. Many of our city developers today are building squeezed-up row houses, in order to make as much money as possible, where the front foot is valued in dollars. But, for all that, the Jamestown developers were doing the very same thing, building sardine-packed row dwellings—only the payment was in English currency.

Inside James Fort that first year the settlers erected streets of "settled" houses, which, because of the small space available within the palisade, must have been of necessity row homes. The current oil painting of James Fort in the Jamestown Museum is all very fine, being based largely on a plan and description of the first settlement by the writer; but it has one great error: the houses are not contiguous to one another, as they were forced to be within the cramped space of the triangular palisade. Four years later, the settlement had two fair rows of timber-framed houses, two storeys and garret high. Even storehouses at Jamestown were constructed in rows. In 1614 there were erected in that settlement three large, substantial storehouses, joined together in length about one hundred and twenty feet, and extending in breadth forty feet.

What appears from a drawing in the Ambler Manuscripts to be an early example of a row dwelling is the "Governor's House" or the "Country House," — the word, country, meaning not countryside, but Colony or Province. This edifice was situated at Jamestown, but it was outside the triangular Fort and upon the so-called "fourth ridge," the highest ground near that fortification. The house was erected some time between the arrival in Virginia of Sir George Yeardley in 1619 and the year 1660. The probable date lies somewhere in the 1620s. The manuscript drawing is crudely drawn and badly torn, but it does indicate a one-and-a-half storey domicile with three chimneys, one in the center and one at each end — making what seems to be a *double* house — a duplex. Excavations of the fragmentary brick remains of the "Governor's House" revealed that it was a brick edifice fifty-three feet long and twenty wide, with a little frame wing at the rear. Unfortunately no trace remained of the central chimney; but at any rate the diggings established that the eastern half had a cellar, while the western section did not — another indication of the double house.

There is an interesting story about the "Governor's House." Those who disagree with the Gregory-Forman theory of the site of James Fort of 1607 being at or near the point below Orchard Run, Jamestown Island, not a half mile up river near the Brick Church, must explain away the conversation recorded in the archives of Virginia for the night of June 23, 1624, at the "Governor's House," Jamestown. Briefly, there were two "fellows" who lurked on that evening under the walls of this building, trying to get inside. They were seen and hailed by sentries on the walls of James Fort. One of the men at the Fort shouted at the two fellows: "Que Vulla?" — evidently stock military vulgar Latin for *Quae Vultis*?, "What do you want?" To which question the two fellows at the "Governor's House" replied that they could not get in because the door was locked. It is obvious that the Fort lay near the Governor's House and not half a mile away.

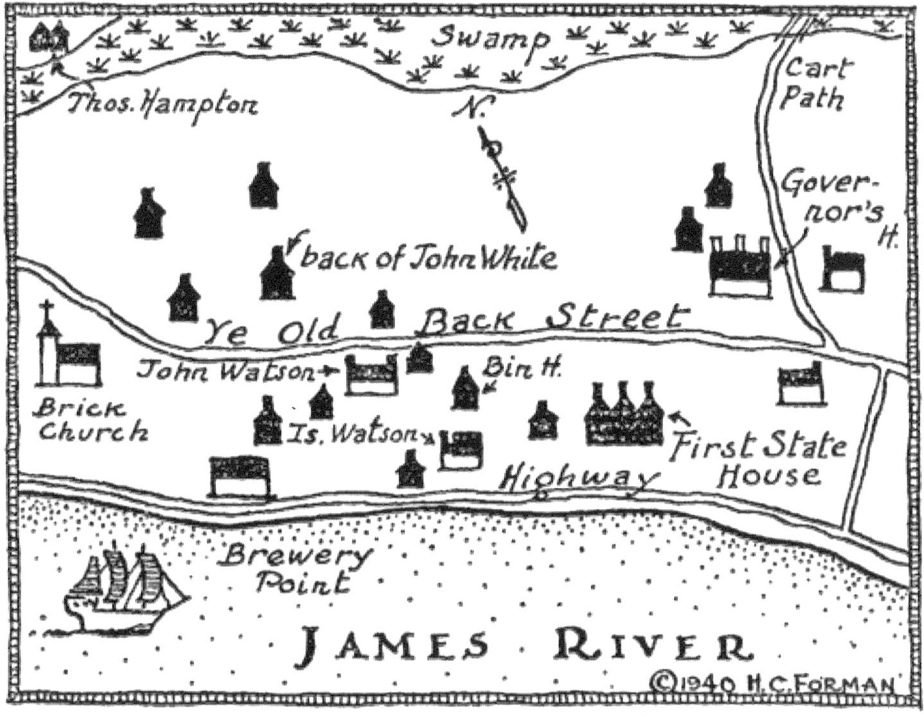

MAP OF THE "NEW TOWNE" AT JAMES CITY.

Illustrating buildings mentioned in the text, and based on a map in the writer's *Jamestown and St. Mary's*

At least by 1623, it was the desire of the Virginia Company of London to build towns in Virginia which would possess a convenient and suitable number of houses, constructed together of brick and encircled by a battlemented brick wall. Exactly in the same way Cecilius Calvert, Lord Baltimore, commanded the first Maryland settlers to lay out row houses in their first settlement.

And also, Jamestown excavations have borne out the fact that the typical city building was usually a row affair. The few rural homes within the city limits may not be classified as "town" houses. There are at least five groups of row houses known at Jamestown, and there are even stock sizes for such groups. Twenty feet by forty, measured on the inside of the walls, were the most common dimensions—an inheritance from British medieval building laws.

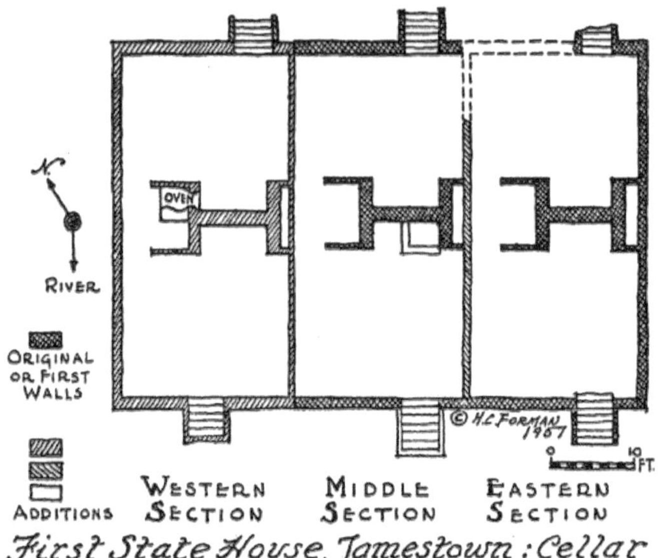

First State House, Jamestown : Cellar

*First State House,
Jamestown: River Front
· Author's Reconstruction*

Perhaps the foremost of the James City row buildings is the group of three brick edifices which comprised the "First State House" in Virginia. The three cellars, their long walls being party walls, were excavated under the direction of this writer and of a colleague. The structure was originally two storeys and garret high. The down-river, or eastern section, and the central portion, were erected about 1635 by Governor John Harvey and were used as the capitol building of the Colony from 1641 for fifteen years. The up-river section was built before 1655 by Sir William Berkeley. But by 1670 the whole pile, with its three front gables facing the James River, had gone up in flames.

The unit floor plan of the "First State House" comprised a "hall-and-parlor" dwelling with back-to-back fireplaces and a very narrow passageway running the length of the building at one side. Now that arrangement formed pretty much the stock plan of the city house in seventeenth-century London, as our researches have disclosed. That the "First State House" was Tudor in appearance is evidenced by the great wealth of medieval wrought-iron hardware found in the ruins: such items as Cock's Head hinges, leaded lattice casements, and great rim locks with eight-inch keys. The roof once carried the medieval "pantile," which is an "S"-shaped clay tile about thirteen inches long, with a nob at one end to catch on to the roofing strips.

Another row example with gables facing the street lay about a thousand feet north of the Brick Church at Jamestown. It comprised two brick buildings with their long sides being party walls; and we have named them the "Double House on the land of Thomas Hampton." Each basement is approximately sixteen feet by twenty-four in size—another stock configuration—which came about as the result of the Virginia Act of 1639. This duplex contained beautiful Delft tiles in the fireplaces, representing figures of Dutchmen at sport and at play.

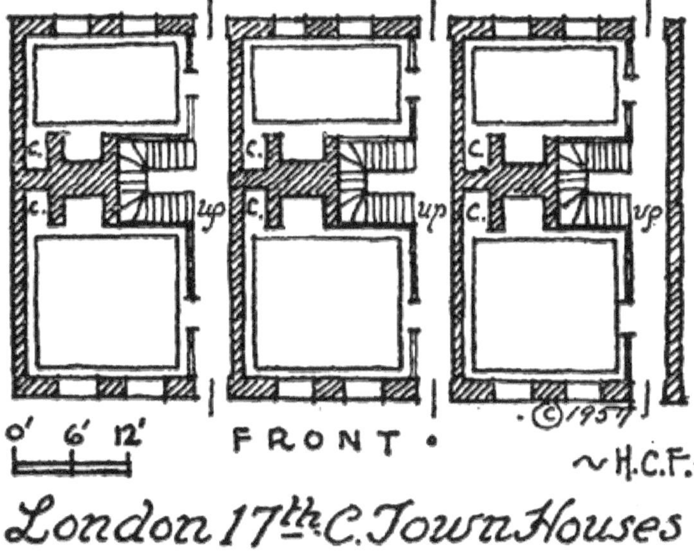

London 17ᵗʰ C. Town Houses

Not all row dwellings had gables across the front; some buildings were joined end to end, their gables party walls. The most important example of such at Jamestown is what we have called the "Country-Ludwell-State House" block of five buildings, situated up river a short distance from the Brick Church. Four of these were private homes, and the fifth was the "Third State House." They were all set up as a result of the Act of 1662 calling for thirty-two brick (row) dwellings, arranged in a square or other form which the Governor should decide. Each dwelling was to be twenty feet by forty on the inside, eighteen feet from floor to eaves, fifteen feet from eaves to ridge measured vertically, and to have a slate or tile roof. Of these four habitations, the two nearest the river had floor plans similar to that of the "First State House," already described, except that the gables adjoined one another.

To delve a little further into the subject of this interesting block, we may note that the other two houses were of the same size as the pair nearer the water, but that they had "flush" chimneys abutting the party walls instead of "central" chimneys with back-to-back fireplaces. These two were also marked by three enclosed porches on their front façades. All four dwellings had "cell" or "aisle" additions at the rear.

Another row house at James City is what we have called the "Double House back of John White's Land," where half the building possessed a large, brick-vaulted, wine cellar, with hundreds of bottles kept within it—a feature indicating a tavern. Let no one think they did not drink at Jamestown: the whole settlement was permeated with taverns and ale-houses.

One of the most recent finds at Jamestown is a triplet or "triplex" row, lying some four hundred feet northeast of the Brick Church. The three dwellings faced south, and each measured twenty by fifty-two feet within the walls. There was the customary back-to-back fireplace on the north wall of each unit; but the easternmost house had an exterior fireplace at its east gable-end, and a square porch room on the south.

As new discoveries are made in this first capital of Virginia, it becomes clearer year by year that the city was full of row buildings, trying to emulate Oxford or Chipping Camden or even the great London herself.

IV. CHURCHES, CHAPELS, AND GLEBES

The medieval Virginia church of the seventeenth century was generally a crossroads shrine set down in or near the middle of a group of plantations. Towns, like James City, also had their own churches, situated on the main thoroughfares. When roads were too bad for traversing, or distances were too great, parishioners built sometimes small fanes called "chapels of ease," nearer their homes than the main parish churches.

The starting point for the Virginia church is at Jamestown, a place which can count five churches, and perhaps more. For brevity we list them:

> 1. The "cruck" church of 1607, the first substantial church, which, according to Smith, was covered by rushes, boards, and earth.

> 2. The timber-framed church of 1610, of Lord Delaware, sixty feet by twenty-four in size, where took place in 1614 the marriage of the Indian princess, Pocahontas, and John Rolfe. This edifice had casements on hinges and, at the west end, two bells.

> 3. Argall's frame church of 1617, fifty feet by twenty, which by 1623 may have been the structure possessing a latticed gallery for ladies, and which needed repairs in 1624.

In connection with this 1617 church, may we digress a moment to mention some contemporary churches outside Jamestown? We have already cited the puncheoned church (c. 1623) on the Eastern Shore. Then there was the Elizabeth City church of 1624, timber-framed, laid upon cobblestone footings, and paved with square tiles; and the wood Hog Island Church of 1628, which measured on the inside twenty by forty feet and which probably had a small tower at the west end. That must have been a tower, because it was not the custom to place a porch at the west end in seventeenth-century Virginia—at least, as far as present research has disclosed. The tower was eight feet wide, but projected only three feet out—big enough, perhaps, to support two or three bells.

To continue the chronology of the Jamestown churches:

4. A wood church, spoken of as "new" in 1636, located next the Reverend Hampton's land, and of which he was the minister. The brick-and-cobblestone footings inside the Brick Church of 1647 at Jamestown may very well have belonged to this "new" wooden church; but they never belonged to Argall's Church, which was located within James Fort, situated half a mile down the James River, near Orchard Run, Jamestown Island.

5. The Brick Church of 1647, of which the original bell tower and foundation are extant.

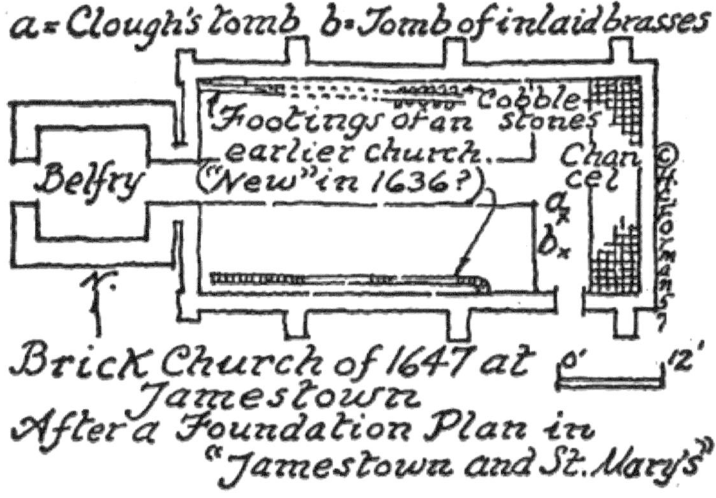

The tower of this Brick Church at Jamestown is of fine old "English" bonded brickwork, with a belt course of Flemish bond. It was built separate from the main body of the church, but was connected to it at the jambs and tops of the interconnecting doorways—as the floor plan shows. The great walls of the belfry are three feet thick, and the roof was probably battlemented or crenellated.

The main entrance doorway in the tower has a plain, round-headed brick arch, the earliest form of brick church door in the Old Dominion.

In 1907 the main body of the church was reconstructed for the Tercentenary Celebration. It is a single nave and possesses some interesting medieval features: buttresses; pointed and mullioned windows; gables of crow-steps or "tabled off-sets"; and a raised tile chancel floor.

The stepped gables were modelled upon those of "St. Luke's Church," often called the "Old Brick Church," Isle of Wight County, Virginia. We are fortunate in having in this country such an excellently-preserved medieval church as "St. Luke's." For years its date was considered "1632"; but the authorities, G. C. Mason and T. T. Waterman, in recent years have assigned to this pile the dates respectively of "1677 or before" and "1682."

Unlike the belfry of the Brick Jamestown Church, the tower of old "St. Luke's" is incorporated into the west gable-end of the building. It, too, probably had a battlemented top, which has now been changed. That the Jamestown belfry is a good deal older than the one at "St. Luke's" is proven by the simplicity of design of the former in contradistinction to the sophisticated appearance of the latter. The "St. Luke's" tower possesses Jacobean brick quoins, a feature imitating corner stones, and an "embryo" or much simplified, triangular pediment, of Jacobean derivation, over the circular-headed doorway.

The buttresses, the crow-stepped gables, the pointed windows at "St. Luke's" are all original medieval features. In fact the great east window of the chancel, made up of eight main lights separated by foliated tracery, is English Gothic, of the style known as "Decorated" or "Geometric," which flourished between 1307 and 1377 in England. A source for this east window is the chancel traceried window at Liscomb Park Chapel (c. 1350), Soulbury, England.

From the foregoing it is obvious that the main body of the "St. Luke's" church preceded the Tudor Style and is "Decorated" Gothic. The tower has Jacobean trimmings. At the same time it is erroneous to call this church "Gothic Colonial." What a mixture! In style it is English Gothic, that is, Gothic of England. It is as much Gothic as "Westminster Abbey" or "Wells" or "Yorkminster." What a multitude of errors is covered by that word "Colonial."

Recent research done at "St. Luke's" has uncovered the original, chamfered, timbered trusses and horizontal tie-beams, which were exposed in the nave; traces of the original gallery at the tower end of the nave which appears to have had balusters of oak; the old wineglass pulpit; and the enclosed porch or vestibule in the first storey of the tower.

Let not the reader think that most Virginia churches in the seventeenth century had towers. Such buildings were usually simple rectangles, occasionally with a porch attached to the long side on the south, in the approved English parish church manner.

Giving an idea how an early church was constructed is revealed in the building specifications of the "Second Hungars Church" (1680), in Northampton County—an edifice which was contemporaneous with old "St. Luke's." Specifications can be pretty dry reading, but this one had a humorous touch or two. It appears that the church wardens contracted with the builder to put up a timber-framed parish church forty feet by twenty, with wall plates ten feet high. Wall plates, by the way, are timbers upon which rafters rest. Of "substantial substance," the framing was to be oak, and the foundation to be locust blocks of wood. The walls and roof were to have planks or clapboards. It is interesting that the upper edge of the roof planks were to be let, or set, into the rafters for strength and tightness. The inside of the church was also to be planked in order to seal off the walls of the "Old Church,"—the "First Hungars Church,"—which seems to have been incorporated, at least in part, in the second shrine. The planks covered the barrel vault, which was called "Arches," situated beneath the roof. Nails, planks, and food were to be furnished to the builder.

One of the excellent contract provisions was that the contractor was to take over no additional work elsewhere, or to leave the works, except upon some great occasion, for a week or two at the most. Upon completion of the job he was to receive ten thousand pounds of tobacco and to have the help of a hand able to work an axe for the space of a month.

The foremost example of Jacobean Style in early ecclesiastical work was the "Second Bruton Church," Middle Plantation, now Williamsburg. It was completed in 1683—that is, soon after "St. Luke's,"—and has been completely demolished. Excavations of its brick foundations revealed that it possessed buttresses on its long sides and at the back. The inside measurements were sixty feet by twenty-four. The main west door—there was no tower—and the chancel door on the side were to be, with minor variations, the sizes of the doors of the Brick Church of 1647 at Jamestown. An old drawing shows that the "Second Bruton Parish Church" had curvilinear gables of the type found at "Bacon's Castle," and the western rose window was flanked by scrolls which were probably formed of hand-cut brick. Both of these features are Jacobean.

Another early doorway, which is plain, round-headed, and of rubbed brick, stands at the "Merchant's Hope Church," Prince George County, and in style it seems to bolster the theory that at least a portion of the existing shrine is of the seventeenth century.

Some believe that brick "Pungoteague Church" on Eastern Shore, originally erected on a cross plan, with a mansard roof, was seventeenth-century in date, but it is the part of wisdom to accept G. C. Mason's belief for valid reasons that the pile was constructed as late as 1738.

That some of these parish churches in Virginia had interiors which were richly furnished is evident from the description of the builder's work on one of them, the frame "Poplar Spring Church," (1677), Gloucester County. Father Time has unfortunately done away with this shrine, but we do know that its walls and ceiling were lathed and plastered, and that the chancel, fifteen feet long, was to be divided from the nave by a wooden *rood screen*—a "Screen to be run Crosse the church," and to have "ballisters."

In the medieval English church the rood screen is the name given to the chancel or choir screen when it supported the "rood," a large cross. It was customary to build such a screen in three parts: a base comprising panelled walls as high as the pews, a middle section with a row of wood balusters set closely together, and a top part of pierced woodwork—that is, traceried work—and heavy cornice.

At "Poplar Spring Church" there were double pews built on each side of the chancel abutting the rood screen. Also set against the rood screen was another double pew, this one between the pulpit in the nave and the screen. The rest of the pews in the church, on both sides of the aisle, were double and had panelled backs. The pulpit itself was hexagonal and a three-decker affair. There was a six-foot space permitted for the reading desk, set eighteen inches above the floor, and for the passage into the pulpit. Half way up were the minister's pew and desk. The church was also the proud possessor of a flowered, crimson, velvet pulpit cloth, a silver communion service, and a drawing of cherubim, presumably upon the altarpiece.

Although it was customary to place wainscoted pews within the chancel, the "Second Lynnhaven Church," of 1692, Princess Anne County, had also in the chancel several benches, which were used by the parish poor.

That all seventeenth-century churches in the Old Dominion were not of brick or wood is shown by the "Second York Church" (1697), now Grace Church, Yorktown, which was constructed of native marl.

The Transitional Style of architecture, which, as we have seen, greatly influenced rural dwellings from about 1680 to about 1730, is marked in the Virginia church chiefly by the doorway designs. The earliest motif of a brick doorway is that plain, round-arched one on the entrance to the Jamestown Brick Church belfry. By 1700, brick doorways were becoming transitional: a good example is that at "Ware Church" (perhaps 1715), Gloucester County, which is flanked by brick pilasters and an arch bounded by a shallow hood—the whole made up of rubbed or gauged brick.

One of the most curious doorways of transitional vintage is the main south entrance to "Yeocomico Church" (1706), Westmoreland County. The door head consists of three brick arches in relief with stucco tympanums or fillings. Of the three, the top arch rests upon the other two—much in the manner that small arches cluster inside a large arch in some English Gothic doorways. But the "Yeocomico" door has the flavor of transitional experimentation.

Apropos of this same "Yeocomico" church, the door itself is a heavy battened door which is Tudor, and which is believed to have been taken from an earlier church (1653) on the same site. At all events, the long vertical panels on the exterior of the door are reminiscent of those at "Christ's Cross," New Kent County, already described. But the "Yeocomico" entrance has an additional medieval feature: a small door or "wicket" within the big door—a feature common to buildings of the Middle Ages abroad.

Most early Virginia churches possessed parsonages, usually on the glebe land and therefore known as "glebes." We have already cited, as an example of the Transition, the "Abingdon Glebe House" (c. 1700), Gloucester County, erected with balancing pavilion wings. Another interesting glebe was specified in 1635 for erection on Old Plantation Creek in Northampton County. Such a building appears to have been of the "hall-and-parlor" variety with a chimney at each end and with a study "outshut" and a buttery "outshut" off each chimney. On the front was an "entry," the familiar little enclosed square porch, and at the rear were a "Kitchinge" and a "Chamber." In size this parsonage was to be forty feet by eighteen, and there were nine feet to the "wall plates," upon which the rafters rested. One could almost make an accurate restoration drawing of this glebe house from the description. But it must have been typical of the minister's house of that day, and the building of a "study" perhaps indicated that religion was then based on learning.

V. STATE HOUSES AND OTHER PUBLIC BUILDINGS

From the records we may learn of many kinds of public buildings, even though their actual remains have disappeared above ground. We know, for instance, of the Tavern or Ale-house (1660) of Thomas Woodhouse at Jamestown, where at one time were made the laws of Virginia. We are cognizant of the Eastern Shore tavern of 1697 where John Cole was licensed to keep an "ordinary" and to retail liquors near the Court House. We have heard of the "quartering house" of 1670 in Accomack County, which was a kind of tourist home for one-night stop-overs. We learn that there were many courthouses in seventeenth-century Virginia, like that of 1690 in Northampton County, which is sketchily described as having one exterior chimney and as being twenty-five feet long. Jails there were, too, like the Westover Prison and Stocks of 1643, which were probably constructed by Theoderick Bland. In Accomack there stood in 1674 a "logg'd" prison, fifteen feet by ten. At Westover, it may be noted, was also a "Brew house."

Also from the records we find mention of the Salt Works of 1676 owned by Daniel and Anne Jenifer and of Darby's Grist Mill of 1668, both in Accomack County; and of the Windmill of 1642 constructed jointly by John Williams and Obedience Robins, "chirugion," in Northampton County.

The Glass House or Factory of 1608 near Jamestown is one building which we do know something about, because of excavations by the National Park Service. It had originally a dirt floor about fifty feet by thirty-seven—a large area. Upon this floor were built three crude stone furnaces and a pot kiln. There was probably an open-walled timber structure with a pitched roof over the large floor and with louvres for the thick smoke to escape through the roof. There is not the slightest evidence for the use of crucks in the present off-site reconstruction of this great pile.

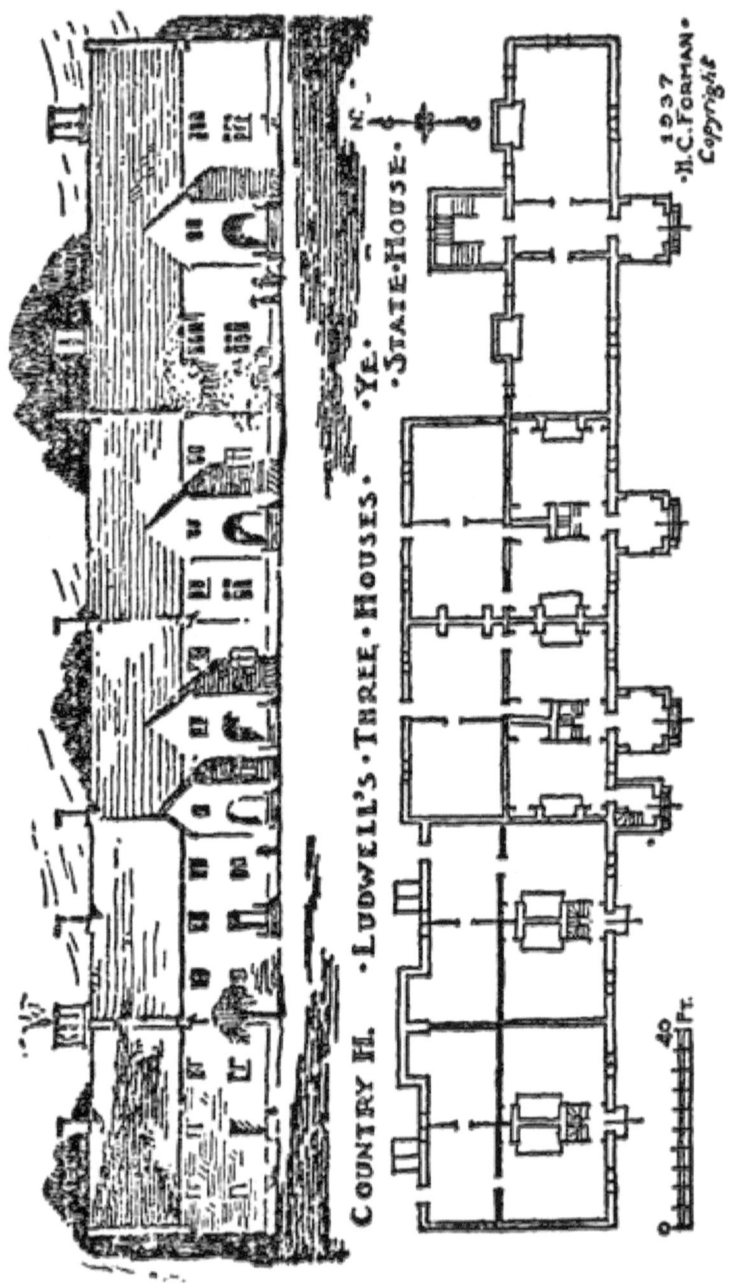

THE COUNTRY-LUDWELL-THIRD STATE HOUSE BLOCK

Author's reconstruction from *Jamestown and St. Mary's* showing four residences and the first American state house to be built specifically as a State House or Capitol.

When we take up the subject of State Houses, we have an excellent example in the "Third State House" at Jamestown, which, as heretofore noted, formed part of the "Country-Ludwell-State House" block of five buildings a little up river from the Brick Church of 1647. Only the foundations of the "Third State House" remain, but from them and from the references in the Virginia records we know pretty much how the edifice looked originally. And it is noted as the first structure in the United States erected as a legislative seat.

Built about 1662 and burned in 1676, the "Third State House" was a medieval cross-house possessing close analogies to "Bacon's Castle" in the general neighborhood, and it rose two full storeys and garret high. There was no basement. The main façade, facing the south and the main body of Jamestown, had a porch and porch chamber, and at the back was a tower which held the stairway—an area which in that day was known as a "Stair Case." In size, the stair tower was about the same as that of the "Brick State House of 1676" in St. Mary's City, Maryland, a cross-building which postdated the Virginia structure by only about thirteen years.

The interior of the "Third State House" must have been impressive. Downstairs were a spacious waiting room and a Court House Room, in which the Governor and his Council met and in which at times Provincial Courts were held. Upstairs were another waiting room and the Assembly Hall or House of Burgesses. The little porch chamber on the second floor was used by His Majesty's Secretary of Virginia, until he was ordered to work in the eastern garret.

The four great rooms in this pile—two down and two up—had huge fireplaces on their long sides. The downstairs fireplaces could burn nine-foot logs. All the ceilings had girders and joists exposed.

After the conflagration of 1676 set by Nathaniel Bacon, the building was rebuilt (1685) on the same site, probably using what brick walls were still standing, to become the "Fourth State House." It is believed that in the rebuilding there was not much change in the design. But it was only natural that some of the rooms should have new uses, so that we find that the lower waiting room was fitted into a Secretary's Office by placing a strong partition under the "second girder" and, because of dampness, by raising the floor two feet up from the ground. To keep persons from breaking in to steal the record books of the Colony in the small storage room next to the Secretary's Office, the windows were barred with iron and had board shutters half an inch thick, with cross-bars.

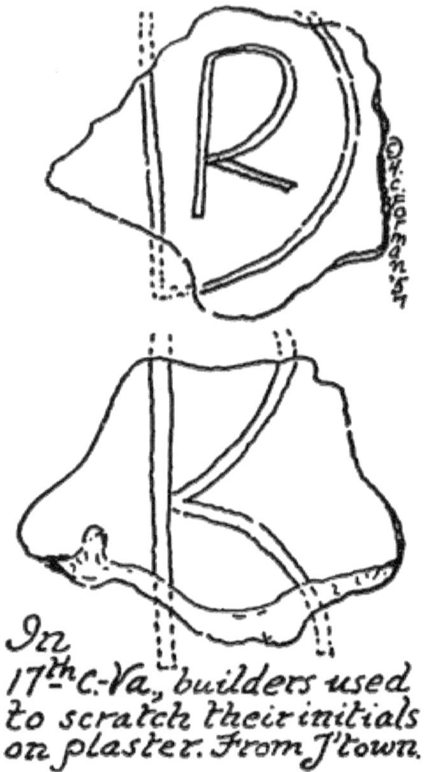

Virginia may well be proud of the design of this "Third State House" at Jamestown, which has recently been the subject of a special restoration study for the Commonwealth by this writer. That legislative seat, built nearly three hundred years ago, was dignified, handsome, impressive, and in fine scale. Through its portals passed in those days the chief figures of the Dominion. Its mullioned and diamond-pane windows, its pantile roof, and its porch and porch chamber gave the fabric a strong medieval flavor.

It is unfortunate that the "Fourth State House" burned on October 31, 1698, through an accident. What kind of an accident the records do not state. Was it a faulty flue, an overturned sconce, or carelessness in lighting a tobacco pipe? We shall probably never know. But the very next year the early capital, Jamestown, which had flourished for ninety-two years, was abandoned in favor of Middle Plantation, "nigh his Majesties Royall Colledg of William and Mary."

Three years before the destruction by fire of the "Fourth State House," the foundation of the "Sir Christopher Wren Building" of William and Mary College was laid down (1695). The shape of the great structure was to have been a quadrangle in the best English tradition of the Middle Ages. Colleges in Britain, as early as the 1200s, were in their general equipment much like monastic establishments, grouped about an arcaded cloister, and were halls of residence for communities of teachers and students.

But in Williamsburg the Wren Building was slow to get started, and has in truth never been completed in the form of a rectangle. By 1705, the year of the first fire, only the front façade and half of the north side had been completed. Consequently, for all intents and purposes, the edifice is an eighteenth-century structure, in spite of its earlier foundation, and belongs more to Classic Williamsburg than to the former era. In more than one respect it paved the way for the Virginia Georgian.

For all that, the style of the original building may be said to be Transitional, with Georgian details, like modillions in the cornice. The main façade, one hundred and thirty-six feet long, is distinguished by a "break-front" or projecting bay on the center, crowned by a steeply pitched gable—the motif being repeated on the courtyard side. According to an old drawing of 1702 the entrance façade had in the center two balconies, one above the other, over the great, arched, front doorway. The hipped main roof is crowned by a "tower" or cupola.

The arrangement of the main roof on the quadrangle side is unique: there is on each side of the central gable a row of hipped roofs. In the early days in Virginia there must have been many a building with a similar row. It is possible that the "First State House" itself had three hips contiguous to one another instead of the three gables which we have drawn herein. At any rate, in order to see existing parallels one has to visit the Bermudas, the Bahamas, or even Great Britain herself.

V

THE RICH HERITAGE OF ARCHITECTURAL DE-TAILS

Although it is true that the vast majority of English buildings in Virginia during the seventeenth century were simple and unadorned, constructed by plain people, there was a large number of structures which had ornate or costly details and exquisite furnishings. What is known about these interesting features is still largely unknown to Virginians, and it is the purpose of this chapter to make mention of some of them.

The richest details known to a seventeenth-century building in the Old Dominion appear to have once upon a time decorated the ceiling of the Great Hall of "William Sherwood's House," built about 1677-80 in Jamestown. The dwelling was a small, brick, storey-and-garret residence built on top of and across the foundation ruins of the old "Governor's House," already described. Mr. Sherwood's Great Hall, seventeen feet by sixteen in size, was rented in 1685 by the Government of Virginia and used as a Council Room by His Majesty's Governor and Council.

Now for the discovery. It was in the excavations of 1935 in Sherwood's neat, brick basement, and in the area immediately surrounding that cellar, that more than fifty thousand fragments of plaster were retrieved. There are still some who do not believe that this plaster work came from Sherwood's House; but like "Kilroy," this writer was there and can vouch for its coming from Sherwood's. In fact we have charts showing exactly where each important fragment of plaster was found, and at what depth below the ground.

The Now Famous Letters from the Jamestown Plaster Garter identified by S. P. Moorehead

At any rate, some of the plaster was colored or frescoed, and much of it was moulded. There were two particular pieces of plaster with raised letters upon them: on one the letters "VI," on the other the letter "Y." What did they mean? This writer invited Mr. Singleton Moorehead, of the Williamsburg Restoration, down to Jamestown Island to view the letters, and he immediately identified them as belonging to the "Garter" of the Royal Arms of Great Britain. In quoting what the Garter states, we have underlined the Jamestown letters, thus: "HONI SOIT QVI MAL Y PENSE." Translated, the words mean, "Evil be to him who evil thinks." There is no doubt that Mr. Moorehead was correct. The tail of the "Q" in "QVI" showed plainly, and the blank space in front of the "Y" indicated that it was a letter by itself. But with the Garter in hand we could identify the other important plaster finds—the masks, roses, leaves, the lion, the hand-and-book, and the ribs, which ordinarily divide a large plaster composition into separate panels—as part of the Royal Coat of Arms.

In England such a ceiling arrangement in plaster was called "pargetry" and was a Tudor manner of decorating an important room. How appropriate to find the Royal Arms of England in the room in Sherwood's which was used by His Majesty's Governor and Council. That was one of the great archaeological finds of America, and the translation of the inscription one of the great interpretations.

The important, widespread, and non-perishable building material of tidewater was brick; and when we take up the subject of seventeenth-century brick-work, we may still with justification hover about the ruins of "William Sherwood's House" at Jamestown as a starting point. It was there were found the largest and most varied collection of rubbed or gauged brick in that capital city. By "gauging" — and we have mentioned the term before in describing certain church doorways, — we mean that the bricks have been cut and finished off by rubbing upon a sandstone. In England by 1660, only about seventeen years before Mr. Sherwood's home was erected, gauged bricks had become widely popular. Such bricks were usually lighter in color than the run-of-the-mill bricks, and were employed on cornices, belt or string courses, quoins at the corners of buildings, and the heads and jambs of openings. They dressed up an edifice in the eye of the seventeenth-century beholder.

Further, we know that in Britain one of the ways of decorating an opening in a late medieval building was to put mouldings on jambs and head of a doorway or of a window. Apropos of Sherwood's at Jamestown, few of us, if any, know that his mansion possessed openings with *ovolo* bricks — bricks rubbed and cut in an egg-shaped ornamental moulding.

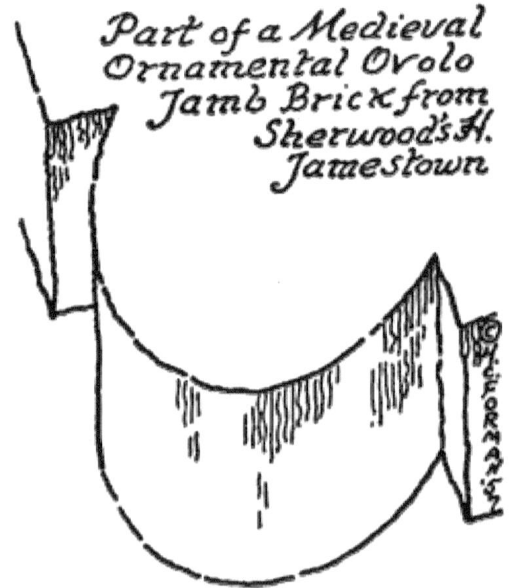

There seems little doubt that Virginians made bricks, even gauged bricks, in their capital and did not bring them from England — popular tradition to the contrary. Several brick kilns have been discovered at Jamestown by the National Park Service. One was a well-preserved, square brick kiln of about 1650, found with arched ovens and with some bricks and tiles in place. The citizens of James City had no difficulty in fabricating all the fancy and ornamental bricks or tiles which they desired.

Virginia brick of the seventeenth century was generally called English brick or English *statute* brick, not because it was brought from England — which it was not—but because its size was regulated by English law. There was another kind of brick used at that time in Virginia, the Dutch brick, made not by Hollanders but by Virginians and English, which was a great deal smaller than the English brick. The Jamestown English brick generally run 9" by 4¼" by 2¼» in size, but the Dutch brick, yellow in color, average 6» by 2½» by 1½».

In the realm of fireplaces, early Virginia had some ornate ones. Old "Fairfield" (1692), Gloucester County, before its destruction, had a mantelpiece of carved marble and some "linenfold" wainscoting. A peculiarity of Gothic carved decoration, the linenfold design was employed in oak panels in imitation of folded parchment or linen. Sometimes in the Old Dominion a rich array of Dutch faïence tiles, five inches square, decorated the sides of a fireplace, as in the "Double House on the Land of the Reverend Hampton," already described. Those tiles, called Dutch, but probably made in England in the Dutch manner, have blue designs upon a milky white surface, and show human figures—Dutchmen—throwing javelins, bowling, or playing games.

In the field of wrought-iron work early Virginia was outstanding. Iron was a common commodity, even as far back as 1610, when the Spanish spy, Don Miguel, wrote from Jamestown to Spain that iron mines, and mines for other metals, were being worked in Virginia. Then, in 1619, Sir Edwin Sandys, Treasurer of the Virginia Company of London, sent one hundred and fifty persons to Virginia to set up three iron works. Glassware, too, was made as early as 1608, at the "Glass House" on Glass House Point, near Jamestown, and was imported into England; but the fragile nature of glass has caused it to endure less well than wrought-iron. Probably much of the best quality ironwork was brought from England: we have record, for instance, of Sir John Harvey in 1639 bringing with him "iron wares to the value of upwards of £45."

The wooden casement window, as well as that of wrought-iron, often gave Virginians a chance to create beautiful and enriched designs. The little metal casement taken from the ruin on the "John Washington Farm" of about 1670 in Westmoreland County measures only 12¾" across and 18½" tall, yet it has a fairly ornate iron plate, punched and cut out in an interesting design, over which is fastened a spring latch-bar, also of a cut-out shape. A ring or pull through which a finger could be slipped to twist a lever against the latch-bar to open the casement was welded to the latch itself. When viewed from the interior of a room, the ornamental fastener was especially effective silhouetted against the light. There was no limit to the fanciful shapes and decorations of such fasteners.

The "First State House," which as we have already noted formed a group of three row dwellings at Jamestown, had in its day probably as much wealth of ornate ironwork as any other building in the Old Dominion. From its ruins came a veritable mine of hardware of good quality, yet rusted. A few specimens may be mentioned here: Cock's Head hinges—a type of "H"-hinge with four heads, the pattern of which harks back to Roman times; an ornamental cupboard latch-lock, made of wrought-iron and steel, with a punched and lobed silhouette, a spring, a pull for turning; and a bar delicately incised with diagonal grooves.

Another bit of hardware from the "First State House" was a pair of decorative cupboard latch-bars, with diagonal grooves, with spear-and-ball terminations at one end and with "V"-shaped notches at the other.

An outstanding example of woodcarving is the folk Jacobean capital with its heart shield and twin volutes at the dwelling, "Christ's Cross," in New Kent. How many other wood sculptures of equal importance have been lost in the almost clean sweep of seventeenth-century Virginia building?

For all that, we know today that the Virginia domicile and edifice sometimes possessed in its details and its decoration an elegance scarcely yet realized in this country—an elegance for which it is necessary to search England to find the proper sources and comparisons.

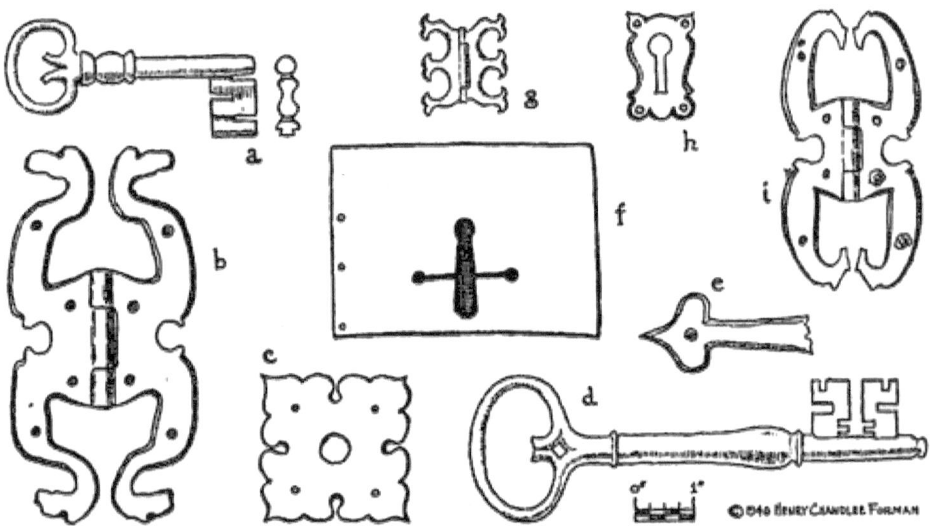

MEDIEVAL DOOR AND FURNITURE HARDWARE FROM JAMES-TOWN

Originally made for *Antiques Magazine*, this drawing shows a. wrought-iron key; b. and i. Cock's Head hinges; c. door-pull escutcheon; d. iron key; e. part of a strap-hinge; f. stock-lock main plate; g. small brass cabinet hinge; h. brass keyhole escutcheon.

VI

EPILOGUE: WHAT HAPPENED TO THE SEVEN-TEENTH-CENTURY STYLES?

When over the fens and marshy slashes of Jamestown Island the eighteenth century dawned in that year of 1700, there were two significant aspects of Virginia architectural history which stand out clearly. Today the first of these aspects is well known, but the second is known only to a handful of persons. They are:

1. The most important style of architecture of the eighteenth century—the pseudo-classical Georgian—was about to make its entrée upon the Virginia scene, with the building of the "Governor's Palace," Williamsburg, begun in 1706.

2. All the styles of architecture, both American Indian and English, which flourished in the seventeenth century carried over—*hung over*—into the eighteenth century, and even into the nineteenth century.

The Georgian Style, of course, was actually English Georgian—Georgian of England—and in Virginia it prevailed from the 1710s to the 1780s—a span of some seventy years. It ushered into the Old Dominion a rage for ballrooms, such as that in the "Governor's Palace," theatres, tea tables, and china. It marked the golden age of the great houses, like "Marmion," "Stratford Hall," "Westover," and "Mt. Vernon."

At the same time in Virginia there existed side by side with the Georgian Style the following five styles of architecture, of which the last four have been identified and named by this writer for convenience:

1. The American Indian Style, which faded away probably in the first quarter of the nineteenth century.

2. The "Hangover" Medieval Style.

3. The "Hangover" Jacobean Style.

4. The Transitional Style, which, as we have seen, prevailed from about 1680 to about 1730.

5. The "Hangover" Transitional Style (after about 1730).

In this way, like a mighty river the four main streams of Virginia architecture in the seventeenth century—American Indian, Medieval, Jacobean, and Transitional—flowed into the eighteenth, to be then joined by the Georgian tributary.

Furthermore, in the nineteenth century the men of tidewater Virginia who put up the buildings in the false medieval style, the copybook, birthday-cake Gothic known as the "Gothic Revival," were not aware of, and took no cognizance of, the true medieval examples existing on their very doorsteps—a "Thoroughgood House" here, a "St. Luke's Church" there. That situation was one of the strange paradoxes of our architectural history.

A few of us in very recent years are just beginning to label those English structures along tidewater which make up the bulk of Virginia architecture in the seventeenth century by the correct name, *Medieval.*

SELECTED BIBLIOGRAPHY

Ambler Manuscripts, Library of Congress, Washington, D. C.

"American Notes," C. E. Peterson, ed., *Journal of Society of Architectural Historians*.

Bruce, P. A., *Economic History of Virginia in the Seventeenth Century*. N. Y. 1895. 2 vols.

Bushnell, D. I., Jr., *Native Villages and Village Sites East of the Mississippi*. Washington, D. C. 1919.

Bushnell, D. I., Jr., *Virginia before Jamestown*. Washington, D. C. 1940.

Caywood, L. R., *Excavations at Green Spring Plantation* (brochure). Yorktown, Va. 1955.

Forman, H. C., *The Architecture of the Old South*. Cambridge, Mass. 1948.

Forman, H. C., "The Beginning of American Architecture," in *College Art Journal*, vol. 6. no. 2. Winter, 1946.

Forman, H. C., "The Bygone 'Subberbs of James Cittie,'" in *William and Mary College Quarterly*, 2nd ser., vol. 20, no. 4. October, 1940.

Forman. H. C., *Jamestown and St. Mary's: Buried Cities of Romance*. Baltimore, 1938.

Forman, H. C., "The Old Hardware of James Towne," in *Antiques Magazine*, vol. 39, no. 1, January, 1941.

Harrington, J. C., *Glassmaking at Jamestown*. Richmond, Va. 1952.

Hatch, C. E., Jr., *The Oldest Legislative Assembly in America & its First State House*. Washington, D. C. Revised, 1947.

Historic American Buildings Survey. Library of Congress. Washington, D. C.

Gregory, G. C., "Jamestown—First Brick State House," in *Virginia Magazine of History and Biography*, vol. 42, pp. 193-199. July 1935.

Lewis, C. M., and Loomie, A. J., *The Spanish Jesuit Mission in Virginia, 1570-1572*. Chapel Hill, N. C. 1955.

Mason, G. C., *Colonial Churches of Tidewater Virginia*. Richmond, Va. 1945.

Moorehead, S. P., "Christ's Cross," in *Virginia Magazine of History and Biography*, vol. 43. January, 1935.

Moorehead, S. P., "The Castle," in *Virginia Magazine of History and Biography*, vol. 42. October, 1934.

Stewart, T. D., "Excavating the Indian Village of Patawomeke," in *Exploration and Field-Work of the Smithsonian Institution in 1938*. Washington, D. C. 1939.

Swem, E. G., *The Virginia Historical Index*. 2 volumes, Roanoke, Va. 1934-36.

Waterman, T. T., *Domestic Colonial Architecture of Tidewater Virginia*. N. Y. 1932.

Whitelaw, R. T., *Virginia's Eastern Shore*. Richmond, Va. 1951. 2 vols.

Yonge, S. H., *The Site of Old Jamestown, 1607-1698*. Richmond 1904.

INDEX

Lector House believes that a society develops through a two-fold approach of continuous learning and adaptation, which is derived from the study of classic literary works spread across the historic timeline of literature records. Therefore, we aim at reviving, repairing and redeveloping all those inaccessible or damaged but historically as well as culturally important literature across subjects so that the future generations may have an opportunity to study and learn from past works to embark upon a journey of creating a better future.

This book is a result of an effort made by Lector House towards making a contribution to the preservation and repair of original ancient works which might hold historical significance to the approach of continuous learning across subjects.

HAPPY READING & LEARNING!

LECTOR HOUSE LLP
E-MAIL: lectorpublishing@gmail.com